THE LOGIC
OF PRIVATIZATION

Recent Titles in
Contributions in Economics and Economic History

Epistemics of Development Economics: Toward a Methodological Critique and Unity
Kofi Kissi Dompere and Manzur Ejaz

Economic Policy in the Carter Administration
Anthony S. Campagna

State Per-Capita Income Change Since 1950: Sharecropping's Collapse and
Other Causes of Convergence
Leonard F. Wheat and William H. Crown

Work and Welfare: The Social Costs of Labor in the History of Economic Thought
Donald R. Stabile

American Trade Policy, 1923–1995
Edward S. Kaplan

Bastard Keynesianism: The Evolution of Economic Thinking and
Policymaking since World War II
Lynn Turgeon

Latin America in the World-Economy
Roberto Patricio Korzeniewicz and William C. Smith, editors

Information Technology as Business History: Issues in the History and
Management of Computers
James W. Cortada

Dollars Through the Doors: A Pre-1930 History of Bank Marketing in America
Richard N. Germain

The Intellectual Legacy of Thorstein Veblen: Unresolved Issues
Rick Tilman

Inequality: Radical Institutionalist Views on Race, Gender, Class, and Nation
William M. Dugger, editor

Mass Production, the Stock Market Crash, and the Great Depression:
The Macroeconomics of Electrification
Bernard C. Beaudreau

THE LOGIC
OF PRIVATIZATION

The Case of Telecommunications in the Southern Cone of Latin America

WALTER T. MOLANO

Contributions in Economics and Economic History,
Number 182

GREENWOOD PRESS
Westport, Connecticut • London

Library of Congress Cataloging-in-Publication Data

Molano, Walter T.
  The logic of privatization : the case of telecommunications in the
Southern Cone of Latin America / Walter T. Molano.
      p.   cm.—(Contributions in economics and economic history,
ISSN 0084–9235 ; no. 182)
  Includes bibliographical references (p.   ) and index.
  ISBN 0–313–30055–0 (alk. paper)
    1. Telecommunication—Southern Cone of South America.
  2. Telecommunication policy—Southern Cone of South America.
  3. Privatization—Southern Cone of South America.   I. Title.
  II. Series.
  HE7964.S68M64   1997
  384′.041—dc20   96–18230

British Library Cataloguing in Publication Data is available.

Library of Congress Catalog Card Number: 96–18230
ISBN: 0–313–30055–0
ISSN: 0084–9235

First published in 1997

Greenwood Press, 88 Post Road West, Westport, CT 06881
An imprint of Greenwood Publishing Group, Inc.

Printed in the United States of America

The paper used in this book complies with the
Permanent Paper Standard issued by the National
Information Standards Organization (Z39.48–1984).

10 9 8 7 6 5 4 3 2

To Mary Katherine.
My pride and joy

CONTENTS

TABLES

ACKNOWLEDGMENTS

Someone once told me that embarking on a dissertation can be one of the loneliest journeys in your life. In one sense that person was right, but that person also failed to acknowledge all of the wonderful people I would encounter and touch during this odyssey.

First of all, I would like to thank Jackie Looney, Peter Lange, and Bob Bates for recruiting me and giving me the opportunity to conduct my studies as a Duke Endowment Fellow. I would like to give special thanks to my dissertation adviser, Alan Kornberg, and the members of my dissertation committee, Bob Bates, Joe Greico, John Aldrich, Beth Simmons, and Tom Smith. I am very grateful to Yair Aharoni for providing focus and guidance during times of theoretical distress. I would also like to acknowledge Deborah Swenson, Ravi Ramamurti, and Paul Gronke for their invaluable support on the statistical section of my work.

I am very grateful to the Social Science Research Council (SSRC) and the Ford Foundation for their resources to perform field research, and to the Tinker Foundation and the Institute for the Study of World Politics for their generous support during the dissertation phase. I would like to also acknowledge the kind people I met in Argentina and elsewhere in Latin America, especially those who were instrumental in conducting my research: Mariano Kruskevich, Maria Julia Alsogaray, Robert Devlin, Lisa Linsely, Rodolfo Teragno, Leonoldo Portnoy, Javier Villanueva, Carlos Acuña, Eduardo Feldman, Miguel von Bernard, Oscar Muñoz, Andrew Tahta, Claudio Miteff, Carlos Killian, Carlos Monroy, Susanna Mansilla, Atilio Boron, Adolfo Canitrot, Daniel Heyman, Bernardo Kosacoff, Marcelo Delmar, Daniel Alexander, José Luis Machinea,

Luigi Manzetti, Adrian Gotuski, Abel Viglione, Ricardo Scheuer, Esteban Skare, Enrique Antonini, Patricio Yanine, Jonas Bergstein, Tania Dmytraczenko, John Marshall, Paco Riso, Alexandra Herrera, Ben Petrazzini, Raimundo Beca, and Luiz Ferreira Borges. I am especially indebted to Flavio and Mary Martinez, who opened their home and provided me with comfort and care.

Last and most important of all, I would like to thank my wife, Mary Beth, for providing me with the love, care, understanding, and support to get through such an ordeal.

1

INTRODUCTION

The 1980s was a decade of political and economic transition in Latin America. The region suffered several major setbacks, leading some social scientists to label the period the "lost decade." Despite this somber characterization, the 1980s marked an important political and economic watershed. The severe foreign debt and fiscal crises, hyperinflation, and capital flight, along with intense pressure from international financial agencies, forced the countries to experiment with more innovative economic reforms. Emerging from the grips of military control, however, the fledgling democracies lacked the political support to implement fundamental economic changes. Instead, they initially focused on short term stabilization programs that addressed only the immediate symptoms, not the underlying structural deficiencies. Unfortunately, these programs failed to provide any long term economic stability. As the young democracies began to mature, however, they developed the strength to launch more substantive reforms.

Bloated public-sector enterprises and staggering fiscal deficits led many multilateral lending agencies to advocate privatization or the sale of public enterprises. Experience with this policy, however, was limited. Only Great Britain and Chile—neither representative of a typical Latin American democracy—had experimented with the policy prior to the late 1980s. Nonetheless, privatization had enormous political undertones because it advocated the dismantling of a social arrangement that was half a century old. The privatization initiative began to accelerate as the Communist economies of Eastern Europe crumbled during the late 1980s and economies around the world began to shrug off the vestiges of government intervention and control.

Privatization also marked a major shift in development strategy: from one based on public ownership and state led growth to one based on private ownership and market led growth. Furthermore, it constituted a major restructuring of rent seeking groups.[1] These groups consisted of special-interest associations that enjoyed special benefits due to their relationship to the government or a government agency. Indeed, experience tells us that privatization has mobilized some of the most powerful political and economic forces within nations, and this has led to the transformation of many societies.

Despite the potential political problems associated with privatization policies, over eighty countries, most in the developing world, had experimented with it by the end of the 1980s (Nankani, 1990). Not surprisingly, privatization policies were not accepted equally across countries and across time. Some governments embraced the policy wholesale while others flirted with the idea, only to abandon it later. Unfortunately, most privatization policies have been studied as *faits accomplis*. Few researchers have looked at privatization as a phenomenon that actually could have varied outcomes. The focus on successful transactions has allowed a wide range of cases to pass unnoticed. Hence, there is a large gap in the understanding of privatization.

While privatization has been implemented across many sectors, one sector stands out. Telecommunications is a field that witnessed a high level of activity, as well as great variances in outcomes across both developed and developing countries. The first privatization of a telephone company occurred in 1981, when the government of Margaret Thatcher initiated the sale of British Telecom. The next sale of a state owned telephone company, however, did not occur until 1984. This was when the Japanese government sold one-third of Nippon Telephone and Telegraph (NTT). The pace of privatization activity increased in 1985; from then until 1988, privatization attempts at the rate of almost one per year. The tempo further accelerated in 1989, when three privatizations were attempted. The pace became even faster during the early 1990s. The privatization outcomes, however, were not uniform (see Table 1). Between 1981 and 1995, twenty-three cases were recorded.[2] Fifteen of the privatizations were accepted, and eight were rejected.

Table 1
Attempted Privatizations, 1981–1995

Country and Company Name	Year	Outcome
United Kingdom (BT)	1981	Accepted
Japan (NTT)	1984	Accepted
Chile (CTC/ENTEL)	1985	Accepted
Jamaica (JTC)	1987	Accepted
Argentina I (ENTEL)	1988	Rejected
Mexico (TELMEX)	1989	Accepted
Venezuela (CANTV)	1989	Accepted
Thailand (TOT/CAT)	1989	Rejected
Argentina II (ENTEL)	1990	Accepted
New Zealand (NZ TELECOM)	1990	Accepted
South Africa (SAPT)	1990	Rejected
Malaysia (JTM)	1990	Accepted
Brazil (TELEBRAS)	1991	Rejected
Colombia (TELECOM)	1991	Rejected
Uruguay (ANTEL)	1991	Rejected
Greece (OTE)	1993	Rejected
Singapore (ST)	1993	Accepted
Peru (ENTEL)	1994	Accepted
Pakistan (PTC)	1994	Accepted
Hungary (MATAZ)	1994	Accepted
India (VSNL)	1995	Rejected
Bolivia (ENTEL)	1995	Accepted
Czech Republic (SPT)	1995	Accepted

The focus is on telecommunications for several other important reasons. It is a sector that has played an important developmental and political role in most countries (Dordick, 1993; Cronin, 1993; and Hudson, 1994). Due to the large economies of scale needed to generate the level of investment required to obtain a viable telecommunications operation, telephone companies are often one of the most important sources of economic activity and employment.[3] The immense capital investments, or sunk costs, needed to set up telecommunication operations force firms to focus on situations where they can obtain large enough returns to recoup their investments. For this reason, the attempts to privatize national telecommunication companies have been so politically controversial. Indeed, failed attempts to privatize telephone companies were major factors in the fall of the Mitsotakis government in Greece and the Alfonsin government in Argentina.

Telecommunications is an industry characterized by rapid technological innovation and externalities. These characteristics have allowed for the formation of strong network externalities that are often missing in many other industries. This concept of critical mass and reciprocal returns in particular sets telecommunications apart from other technologies or utilities. On the one hand, these characteristics allowed telephone companies initially to develop along generally similar paths, thus making them highly comparable units. On the other hand, lack of investment and poor management allowed these firms to decay to the point where the quality of service was inadequate. Unfortunately, this occurred at the same time that advancements in telecommunications technology were unfolding in the industrialized world. New changes such as mobile communications and digital data transmission, proved to be significant contributors to improved efficiency and economic growth. But countries needed an infusion of capital to implement the changes (Wellenius and Stern, 1994). Thus, conditions were set for cross sectional change.

Another reason why studying the privatization of telephone companies is important is the insight that can be gained from examining the process of selling the telecommunications company. Since the telephone company is often the most important asset to be sold, the privatization can reveal much information about the country's approach to economic reform and development. It can shed light on the country's development priorities, help reveal the underlying political power groups that support or oppose reform, and help demonstrate the country's commitment to economic development.

The last reason is related to the sheer magnitude of privatization activity in the telecommunications industry. In 1991, the sale of telecommunications companies accounted for over $7 billion of the $50 billion in global assets that were privatized (*Institutional Investor*, 1992). Indeed, the rapidly changing nature of technology in telecommunications equipment and services generated intense demand for privatized telephone companies. Wellenius (1994) estimated that telecommunications privatizations could absorb an estimated $145–$150 billion by the end of the century, thus becoming an important phenomenon that needs to be understood. The changes in communication technology removed the natural monopoly characteristics of the telecommunications industry that demanded that only one firm be allowed to operate in order to allow a profitable environment, and led to greater competition in the telecommunications sector. State companies were no longer able to dominate the telecommunications industry due to dramatic changes in microwave, fiber optic, and computer technology. These changes revolutionized the telecommunications sector from one of sunk costs and monopoly rents, or rich returns due to exclusive, noncompetitive relationships, to a more flexible infrastructure with higher levels of competition. Hence, firms had to compete in more of a market setting.

After revamping their domestic markets, telephone firms in the Organization for Economic Cooperation and Development (OECD) began to compete on a global basis and were forced to look for new markets in order to increase their global market share and survive (Sandholtz, 1993). The demand for telephone companies in the developing world focused on the expansion of global franchises. Despite the prevalence of decayed capital equipment, the new owners sought to expand market share. Faced with cut throat competition in their home markets, they turned these privatizations into lucrative concessions that allowed the companies to quickly recoup their capital investment while guaranteeing a high level of return during the period of exclusive control (usually five to fifteen years). This made the demand for privatized telephone companies very high, and soon the acquisitions fervor spread even to seemingly worthless telephone companies in the developing world.

Companies in the developing world had what decayed systems, most of them discarded as soon as the new owners could install modern equipment. What was really coveted was not the actual assets but the franchise. With the opportunity to expand the penetration of these markets and to capture high-margin business activities in information services, major telephone companies were willing to pay large sums for these antiquated systems. Nonetheless, despite the high demand for these assets, several attempts to privatize telephone companies were rejected by these capital-hungry countries. Indeed, this phenomenon appears to be counterintuitive and irrational, thus requiring further analysis. Finally, telecommunications was selected as the industry to be studied because it demonstrated variation in the dependent as well as the independent variables across a wide range of cases.

THEORETICAL APPROACH

It is clear that privatization is an important issue. Many researchers have acknowledged this fact, but few theoretical insights have been gained. Privatization research has dealt mainly with three aspects of the transformation. There has been important focus on the microeconomic issues. For example, some researchers have analyzed the impact of divestiture on firm efficiency and performance. Other researchers have focused on macroeconomic factors, such as the net impact on foreign debt and productivity levels. Political scientists have studied the institutional dimensions of privatization and have examined the impact of regulatory structures and depth of local capital markets. While most researchers have analyzed the effect of privatization on society, there has been a dearth of analysis of the actual process of change. This study departs from the standard assumption that all privatizations will be accepted; instead, it looks at all of the possible outcomes. Hence, it poses two important questions. First, given the fact that a country wants to privatize a company, what are the initial conditions that may lead a government to pursue or abandon privatization? Second, what are the economic and political conditions for the public to support the initiation and the implementation of privatization policies?

The basic premise of this study is that the initiation and implementation of privatization policies hinge on the ability of the political leaders to control the extensive bargaining process during the divestiture of state-owned companies. This process starts with the initiation of the policy, and follows through the specific formulation of the privatization initiative, and ends with the implementation of the sale. Failure to control the privatization process may expand the conflict beyond the scope of the original participants and result in its failure at any one of the stages. This theoretical framework is loosely based on Schattschneider's (1960) fourfold schema used to analyze the political dynamics involved in the implementation of U.S. economic programs. Schattschneider proposed that the formation of economic policies was somewhat controversial, and that the outcome of every conflict was determined by shifts in the relative balance of power the inherent balance of power between the central groups. Schattschneider also proposed that the most important role of the politicians was to control the scope of conflicts. He argued that the political actors at the center of any conflict help determine the outcome by controlling the scope of participation. Hence, conflicts were won as a result of the contestants' ability to increase or restrict involvement by external actors or groups. Given the conflictual nature of privatization policies, the Schattschneider framework is quite appropriate.

Several researchers have found conflict to be a central characteristic of privatization policies. An extensive analysis of the phenomenon by Beinen and Waterbury (1989) found that certain groups were consistently opposed to the policy. They included labor unions, civil servants, and the military. Indeed, all of these interest groups have derived high rents from their exclusive relationships with state enterprises—especially in the telecommunications sector. Since this analysis narrowly focuses on telecommunications, I include businesses that provide equipment, supplies, and services to the telecommunications state owned enterprises (SOEs); opposition political parties; and consumers.

Privatization is a very broad concept with myriad dimensions. Thus, it is not surprising that many previous attempts to analyze the phenomenon have been unsatisfactory. I attempt to avoid some of the earlier pitfalls by delimiting the phenomenon through the use of two central assumptions. First, selling state assets is a product of the political bargaining between the political leadership and organized groups. Second, the government represents the selling interest during the bargaining process, while interest groups try to arrive at an agreement that maximizes their rents.[4] Since the government has initiated almost every recorded privatization attempt, I will assume that it seeks to maximize the salability of the company by shifting substantial rents away from interest groups that have dominated the company. For example, the government may guarantee contracts or jobs in other government activities in exchange for the termination of jobs or contracts in the SOE that is being privatized. This work uses the privatization attempts in the telecommunications sector of Southern Cone countries to narrowly examine the political and economic aspects of privatization policies. The case studies focus on the attempts by four Latin American countries—Argentina, Brazil, Chile, and Uruguay—to sell their telecommunication companies (see Table 2).[5]

Table 2
Privatization Attempts in Telecommunications

Ratified Transfer	Rejected Transfer
Chile 1985	Argentina 1988
Argentina 1990	Uruguay 1991
	Brazil 1991

The emphasis on Latin American cases is attributed to the fervor with which the region adopted privatization as a policy (Devlin, 1992). In fact, during 1991, a total of $50 billion in state-owned assets was sold to the private sector—with 30% of the transactions in Latin America. This high level of transactions transformed the region into a virtual laboratory for privatization analysis. Indeed, Latin America has taken the lead in almost every level of privatization activity. Table 3 illustrates the global leadership that the region has assumed. It shows the growth the region undertook as a percentage of global privatization value in 1988 and 1992.

Table 3
Changes in Total Privatization Values

REGION	1988 VALUE	1992 VALUE
Europe	11%	12%
Britain	12%	2%
Latin America	6%	35%
Eastern Europe	0%	32%
Japan	58%	0%
Asia	8%	16%
Other	5%	3%
Total	100%	100%

Source: The Economist, 1993

The selection of the four cases was based on several factors. The first was that the countries in the Southern Cone of Latin America have over two-thirds of the population and domestic product of the region. It is probably the most representative group of countries in South America. The second reason was due to the countries' similar pattern of social, economic, and political development, along with their varying experiences in privatizing their telecommunications SOEs. The third reason was the wave of privatization attempts in the region. The Southern Cone stands out from Eastern Europe, Asia, and Africa, through its attempts to privatize state-owned telephone companies within a short period of time (five years). This study considers a privatization attempt to have occurred from the moment that the executive branch introduces legislation to allow the privatization of the state-owned telephone company. This, of course, omits plain industry inquiries, or trial balloons, made to test market sentiment and salability.[6]

These factors allowed the use of a sample set with a cohesive set of independent variables, but with variance in the dependent variables. For example, Chile's divestiture of CTC was implemented without any societal conflict
and with low transparency. In other words, the fact that there was little known
about the privatization process did not create any social problems. At the same
time, Brazil quietly debated privatization but the process never emerged from
preliminary stages. Uruguay had a heated public debate and the issue was re-
ferred to a general plebiscite, which rejected it. Although the Mexican case
was an interesting privatization of telecommunications, the Argentine case was
a better fit. The Mexican government privatized the phone company (Telmex)
on the first attempt, whereas Argentina attempted to privatize its telecommunication company twice. The first attempt was vetoed by the legislature, but the
second time it was ratified. This case is of special significance because it provides two different outcomes, and thus it is possible to control for various other
factors that may have affected the other privatization attempts. Although I
would like eventually to expand my analysis to Mexico, finite resources have
forced me to choose between the two cases. Nonetheless, I emphasize that this
research project does not select cases based on the privatization outcomes and is
in line with the suggestion made by King, Keohane, and Verba (1994) not to
sample on the dependent variable.[7] Hence, this study poses three questions on
privatization outcomes.[8]

Q1:   How does the microeconomic performance of a state-owned telephone com-
        pany impact the likelihood that a privatization program will be approved?

Q2:   How does the macroeconomic condition of the privatizing country shape its
        privatization policies?

Q3:   How does the political environment affect the implementation of privatization
        policies?

        The first question looks for factors that explain how the variance in
privatization outcomes is explained by firm-level factors, such as efficiency and
performance. The second question looks for explanations of how country-level
factors, such as gross domestic product (GDP) or economic growth, fiscal performance, and the level of foreign debt, impact privatization outcomes. The
third question asks whether the formulation and initiation of privatization
policies depend on the political situation. These questions lead to a structure
consisting of cases that examine the microeconomic, macroeconomic, and political factors shaping privatization policies. These sections are then followed
by a section that employs a quantitative analysis of the three approaches to statistically examine their explanatory power.

MICROECONOMIC FACTORS

It is important to review the two major reasons why the microeconomic approach takes on a central role in this research. In the first place, efficiency was a major factor behind the state's nationalization of many telephone companies. During periods of disturbances to the international economic system, such as the world wars, severe recessions, oil shocks, and debt crises, developing countries found themselves cut off from physical and financial capital. Foreign ownership of telephone companies exacerbated the problem. In order to apply a smoother and more efficient approach to their telecommunications operations, many countries decided to nationalize their telephone companies. Indeed, there were important political considerations behind such a decision, but efficiency was also used as the principal argument.

The other reason for looking at the microeconomic argument is the technological changes that occurred in the industry. As stated earlier, radical changes in telecommunications technology during the 1970s and 1980s revolutionized the industry. These changes reduced many of the economies of scale that were present in the sector during its early years. Furthermore, the use of computer technology allowed the explosion of high-margin information services that could be provided by telephone carriers. Developing countries, however, lacked the capital resources and management expertise to implement these crucial changes that could help revitalize the economy. At the same time, major telephone companies from developed countries desperately combed the world for telephone franchises. Large telephone companies from the developed world disregarded the condition of telephone companies in the developing world. Their only concern was to capture a monopoly franchise for a period that would then allow them to build an impenetrable share of the highly lucrative information services market. This created high demand for telecommunication SOEs. Nonetheless, not all countries were able to divest their state companies; therefore, this chapter uses the microeconomic approach to determine whether company-level factors could provide some insight into this phenomenon.

A survey of the microeconomic literature on privatization focuses on the operating inefficiencies of SOEs and the role of the state. Jones, Tandon, and Vogelsang (1990) argued that studies of privatization programs should be performed only through microeconomic analyses of the divested firms.[9] They suggested that privatization programs were designed to improve the general welfare through more efficient operations, but successful candidates for privatization are only those firms that could improve efficiency through a change in ownership. In other words, companies that performed well, as demonstrated by financial, technological, and service characteristics, would be less likely candidates for divestiture than operations that were relatively inefficient and performing poorly. One can then infer that countries with relatively inefficient telephone companies would be more likely to approve privatization-enabling legislation than countries with relatively more efficient operations.[10]

An important component of the microeconomic analysis has been the role of the state in the management of SOEs. Researchers argued that the evolution of companies under state control hindered competition and encouraged inefficient operations. Much of this literature originated in the "public choice" school of thought. Scholars argued that publicly owned enterprises were less efficient than private enterprises because in the former property rights and rights to profits were more diffused, while in the latter they were more clearly defined, thus encouraging greater efficiency (Ott, 1991). Leyden and Link (1993) suggested that civil servants focused not on efficiency but on using the SOEs to increase income redistribution and political perks. Therefore, the more politically controlled an SOE was, the less efficient it was. Bös and Peters (1991) also argued that managers of public firms put less effort into achieving efficient operations because their monitoring and incentive structures were not based on efficiency-maximizing factors. Hence, they concurred with Leyden and Link and reasserted that the greater the political control, the lower the level of efficiency.

Beca's (1991) study of Latin American phone companies suggested a format for examining efficiency on a comparative basis. He suggested that it should consist of an analysis of the firm's history as well as an examination of its performance, investment, and technology. This is congruent with Levy and Spiller's (1993) analysis of privatization. They found that the use of investment levels, capital allocation, and technical parameters helped establish a telephone company's level of efficiency.[11]

Therefore, the micro level literature on privatization suggested two things. First, by definition, it suggested that the unit of analysis for privatization should be at the firm level. Second, it suggested that efficiency criteria should be used to evaluate how likely a candidate a firm is for privatization. Last, it suggested a format to examine the industry on a comparative basis.

MACROECONOMIC FACTORS

Although the microeconomic approach provides fundamental insight into the forces behind the privatization process, the intense focus on firm efficiency limits the analysis by downplaying the importance of macroeconomic factors. The consensus among most researchers working on company-level issues is that the macroeconomic impact of privatization should be realized by the increased efficiency of the firms that are sold. Fortunately, not all social scientists studying the process of privatization agree with this assumption. Researchers specializing on the process of development argue that privatization initiatives are really driven by country-level factors. They suggest that the focus of privatization analysis should be expanded beyond the microeconomic level, a wider scope where more pertinent variables can be used to explain the process.

One group that examined the impact of government budgetary dynamics on the privatization process was led by Vernon (1988), who argued that there was a strong link between privatization and fiscal performance in developing countries. He suggested that privatization policies were motivated by the tendency of developing countries to run large deficits. Since these countries were acutely short of hard currency, they resorted to auctioning off their most salable public assets. Vernon argued that these countries selected target companies for privatization on the basis of the prices they would command on the international market; therefore, the companies selected were often the best or the most efficient. This observation went against the microeconomic expectations that suggested efficient companies would be the least likely candidates for divestiture.

Beinen and Waterbury (1989) suggested that fiscal deficits were driving privatization policies; however, they argued that the losses generated by SOEs were the reason why developing countries were accumulating large budget deficits. A study by Austin, Wortzel, and Coburn (1986) substantiated this claim by finding that SOEs in Latin America accounted for almost 25% of their gross domestic product (GDP). The assertion was further underscored in a study by Cook and Minogue (1990), who found that SOE deficits averaged almost 4% of GDP in developing countries.

The financial drag generated by SOEs grew exponentially as the debt crisis of the 1980s accelerated and foreign capital inflows declined. Devlin (1992) showed that company deficits not only debilitated the weakened budgetary mechanisms but also compounded the situation by creating inflationary pressures. Pinheiro and Schneider (1993) suggested that states were forced to jettison their holdings in SOEs and that privatization was the quick solution to addressing the fiscal crises. They developed a model showing that privatization supplied countries with a lump-sum revenue that could temporarily offset the fiscal deficit while providing their governments with added income to continue funding politically enhancing social policies.

Another group of social scientists studied the role of foreign debt on the privatization process. Ramamurti (1992) found that many privatization programs in developing countries were motivated by large debt burdens. His statistical study showed a significantly high level of correlation between debt levels and the total number of privatizations. He reasoned that countries shed some of their SOEs to alleviate debt loads. Other social scientists analyzed the borrowing appetites of SOEs. Wellons (1987) found that not only did SOEs account for over one-third of the money borrowed on the Eurocurrency market during the late 1970s, but also that several Latin American governments were not even aware of the borrowing that was being done by state companies until after they defaulted on foreign obligations and the governments were forced to assume the outstanding debts.

Indeed, the lending trends of the late 1970s and early 1980s were reversed in 1982, when commodity prices slumped, interest rates increased, and the industrialized world entered a deep recession. Capital flows to Latin America peaked in 1981, then declined dramatically in the following years.

Hence, countries facing drastic reductions in their capital inflows had to find alternative financial solutions.

A third, and last, group of researchers examined the role of international lending agencies, especially multilateral organizations, in the privatization process. Hemming and Mansoor (1988) and Nellis and Kikeri (1989) argued that debtor nations adopted privatization programs to demonstrate their commitment to stabilization programs. Przeworski (1991) noted that privatization was an almost universal part of recent economic reform programs due to the impetus of international financial institutions. Williamson (1983), Aylen (1987), Babai (1988), and Martin (1994) suggested that multilateral lending agencies, such as the World Bank, the IMF, and the Interamerican Development Bank (IDB), used various methods to pressure developing countries into adopting privatization programs. Lastly, Armijo (1994) argued that the enticement of future loans and grants encouraged many developing countries to sell their state-owned companies. She found that the mechanism to do this was through conditionality clauses that stressed privatization.[12] Therefore, the macroeconomic literature has expanded the scope of privatization analysis beyond the issues centering on firm efficiency. It suggests that three country-level factors—fiscal deficits, debt, and multilateral lending agencies—are the key considerations in the divestiture process.

POLITICAL APPROACH

Like the economic literature, the political literature on privatization has been wide-ranging and varied. Some political scientists focused on the institutions that shaped privatization policies. Some scholars studied the institutional factors, such as the formal rules, agencies, and regulations, that allowed governments to conduct privatization programs (North, 1992; Levy and Spiller, 1993; and Hill and Abdala, 1993). Other researchers analyzed the peripheral institutions needed to handle the divestiture of state assets (Cook and Kirkpatrick, 1988; Ikenberry, 1993; Savas, 1987, and Hanke, 1987). Although institutional analysis could provide important insights into the process of privatization, many of these institutional analyses examined only the organizational differences between countries, resulting in limited theoretical insights.

Recently some studies have refocused their attention on the political dynamics shaping the process of privatization and economic adjustment. Duch's (1991) study of privatization programs in the OECD countries suggested that political structures helped explain the variation in privatization outcomes. He observed that both liberal and conservative political parties introduced privatization initiatives, but implementations were more likely to occur in pluralist open political systems such as the United Kingdom. He found that corporatist closed political systems like Germany were the least likely to implement privatization policies.

Petrazzini (1993), however, applied Duch's format to developing countries and came to the opposite conclusion. He found that governments with open systems were less likely to implement privatization strategies than those with closed systems. Petrazzini explained this phenomenon by arguing that developing countries were not as responsive to the demands of the business sector as developed countries. Yet, analyses have shown that the business sector has been one of the most important groups in shaping privatization policies. Therefore, there has to be a better explanation that incorporates an analysis of the political actors and institutions involved in the privatization process. While no single literature addresses the issue, a theoretical framework can be pieced together from the wide assortment of literature that has analyzed development, presidentialism in Latin America, and the dynamics between economic groups and U.S. presidents.

The role of interest groups during the process of economic transformation has been studied by a wide range of development specialists.[13] Beinen and Waterbury (1989) argued that economic reforms in developing countries often depend on the process of interest aggregation. Mann, Lenway, and Utter (1993) suggested that the privatization of large state-owned enterprises was vitally important to a wide range of interest groups because the new company structures would influence future resource allocations, employment levels, and national output. Furthermore, Haggard and Webb (1994) suggested that economic reform programs could not be fully consolidated unless they had adequate political support from the major interest groups in the country.

Other analyses of structural economic reform programs found that the groups opposed to privatization policies were somewhat consistent across countries. Austin, Wortzel, and Coburn (1986) found that groups such as suppliers, labor unions, and government bureaucrats consistently opposed most privatization programs. Often their opposition tactics delayed, hampered, or even prevented the initiation or formulation of privatization policies, but their ability to shape the process usually depended on their capacity to put countervailing pressures on the government (Nelson, 1990). This capacity often hinged on the groups' cohesiveness and their ability to organize and mobilize resources.

Indeed, the literature on privatization has provided much insight into the role of interest groups in the process of economic change, but it has not provided much light on the role of the national executive. Therefore, we turn to the literature on presidentialism to gain a better understanding of the power of the national executive in Latin American countries.

The presidentialism literature stems from a debate initiated by Juan Linz in 1990 on the perils of presidential systems. His premise was that presidential systems often induce a destructive competitive environment that prevents more coordinated policy outcomes. Linz argued that Latin American countries could be better served by parliamentary systems, because of their power-sharing and coalition-forming characteristics, instead of what he termed the "winner-take-all" logic of presidential systems. The debate also suggested that the transition to democracy played an important role in establishing the power of the president to implement major policy changes.[14] The application of the presidentialism literature to this study is appropriate because of its intense attention to Latin American cases; yet it also provides a fundamental format that can be applied to the study of other political institutions because it is focused on the capacity of political leaders to implement policies. Hence, it can be applied to, for instance, parliamentary governments. Furthermore, some studies on parliamentary governments have focused on the non-majoritarian governments that provide a more dynamic role for the chief executive in handling interest groups and coalitions (Strom, 1984).

In order to establish the power of the national executive, researchers have identified three important factors. The first is the support the president has in the Congress (Horowitz, 1990; Mainwaring, 1993; and Shugart and Carey, 1992). Failure to have a majority in the Congress has often led to confrontational relations between the congress and the executive, thus delaying or hampering economic reforms.[15] A second important factor is the overall economic environment of the country. A perception of crisis may provide policymakers with greater freedom to implement the reforms necessary to rescue the country (Haggard and Webb, 1994). A third factor is the amount of time since the inauguration of the new administration. Studies have suggested that national executives enjoy a honeymoon period in the early part of their administrations that allows them greater discretion in implementing major policy changes (Douglas, 1990; and Haggard and Webb, 1994).[16] Hence, it is important emphasize that timing and speed become crucial to the president's political power.

Although the Latin American and the development literature have contributed important theoretical insights into the role of interest groups and national executives in the process of economic change, they have not addressed the dynamic interplay between these two forces, especially in an economic policy setting. Nonetheless, the cases have shown that each of the two factors cannot serve on their own. It is true that interest groups play an important role in influencing economic policy; however, national executives have been able to stem their power long enough to achieve the implementation of important economic reforms. Fortunately, the literature on U.S. politics has provided some analysis of this type of condition.

Schattschneider (1960) created a framework to study conflicts between U.S. national executives and economic groups. It was based on the assumptions that conflictual situations were narrowly monopolized by the parties immediately concerned and that contests between groups were usually won by the groups that control the scope of the conflict. By applying his observation to presidential systems, he argued that the role of the executive was to control the political process. The executive controlled the number of parties in the conflict by providing side payments to parties to remain outside the dispute. This observation is consistent with the literature on collective action (Olson, 1971). Olson suggested that leaders faced with finite resources needed to limit the number of parties in the core group in order to provide some form of coordinated outcome.[17] Schattschneider also suggested that the weak party in the contest, not the strong, would appeal to the general public for relief, thus expanding the scope of the conflict and increasing the size of the group.[18]

Schattschneider's analysis, however, covered more than the interplay between the national executive and interest groups. In expanding his analysis, he found that the relationship between the two principal actors was constrained by the institutional environment. For example, he noted that one-party systems were very successful in limiting the scope of conflicts because there were no established opposition structures to absorb dissident groups.

Furthermore, according to a Schattschneider-type of framework, the role of the privatizing administration is to limit the scope of the opposition. It can accomplish this feat through many strategies, including making side payments to individual interest groups. Of course, the ability of the national executive to accomplish this objective depends on the political strength it enjoys with the public and Congress. As noted by Schneider (1992), compensating interest groups for their cooperation can be very costly in political and economic terms; therefore, the administration must have a solid foundation to make large reallocations of political and economic capital. A definite measure of political strength is the support the administration has in Congress; specifically, this can be measured by the percentage of the legislative body that has the same political party affiliation as the president. Another indicator is the administration's time in office. National executives often enjoy higher levels of power during the early part of their term. This time period is usually known as the honeymoon. Some presidents use this time period to implement controversial policies. Therefore, a simple model begins to emerge from this framework that pits the national executive or government against interest groups. Differences in the relative power structures of the two sides will provide insight as to whether a privatization policy will be implemented. Therefore, Schattschneider suggested a basic theoretical framework that incorporates all of the components that we have identified as being fundamental to the political analysis of economic change: interest groups, national executives, and institutions.

Hence, by assimilating the concepts gleaned from the political literature on development and presidential systems, we can create a conceptual framework based on several explanatory factors. We can arrange the two principal actors along two axes: the national leadership attempting to implement the privatization policy and the organized groups opposed to the initiative. Each side can then be categorized as weak or strong. Unfortunately, developing countries tend to have relatively weak and fragmented political institutions. As a result, political leaders are often forced to resort to more politicized policy-making. Therefore, this classification leads to a use of variables that measure the power of political groups and the national executive, such as the cohesion and size of the opposition group, the national executive's congressional support, and time in office. The categorization of the relative strength may, however, be hard to quantify and may require a closer reading of the facts.

The analysis will also include the role of institutional rules in shaping the national executive's ability to implement policy options. Institutions become particularly important if the power balance between the two principal actors is relatively equal. In the absence of a strong, dominant party, institutional rules could play an important role in shaping the outcome.[19] Nonetheless, the conceptual framework may allow us to understand the process of economic change and establish a set of expectations. Hence, the use of a two-by-two matrix allows a simple presentation of the framework (see Table 4).

Table 4
Political Framework for the Implementation of Privatization Policies

	Weakly Organized Interests	**Strongly Organized Interests**
Weak Leadership	Type I	Type II
	Both sides evenly matched. Government is too weak to control process.	Organized interests united in their demands. Government is weak and seeks wider debate.
	Institutions: major role	Institutions: minor role
	Result: stagnation	Result: rejection
Strong Leadership	Type III	Type IV
	Leadership uses carrot-and-stick approach to alter rent structure. Interests try to expand the scope of the debate.	Both sides very strong. Negotiations conducted in private.
	Institutions: minor role	Institutions: major role
	Result: implementation	Result: no bidders

Type I: Weak Government/Weak Interest Groups. This situation involves both a weak national executive and weak interest groups. Interest groups are too divided to make a cohesive set of demands on the government. The government lacks the political strength to restrict other groups from entering the debate. Although the outcome may be stagnation, the absence of a dominant party to tip the balance of power may allow institutional rules to play an important role in forcing the outcome. The case that most strongly reflects this situation was the privatization attempt of Telebras in Brazil.

Type II: Weak Government/Strong Interest Groups. In this situation, interest groups are well united and organized in their opposition to the privatization initiative. The government however lacks the congressional support and resources to control the process. In an attempt to change the balance of power, the administration may appeal to the general public for support through increased public participation and open hearings on the privatization program. The initiative, however, will probably be defeated. Given the strong imbalance of power, the institutional rules may play a lesser role. Examples of this situation are the first attempt to privatize ENTEL in Argentina and the privatization of ANTEL in Uruguay.

Type III: Strong Government/Weak Interest Groups. In this situation, the balance of power is reversed from Type II. The interest groups are poorly organized and divided in their demands. The government has strong congressional support and ample resources to control the process. In an attempt to change the balance of power, interest groups may appeal for mass support. If the government is successful in regulating the struggle between itself and the interest groups, it should be able to implement the privatization. The imbalance of power may limit the impact of institutional rules on the outcome. Examples of this situation are the second attempt to privatize ENTEL in Argentina and the privatization of CTC in Chile.

Type IV: Strong Government/Strong Interest Groups. In this situation, both principal parties are relatively strong. The privatization deal, however, may be too expensive for interested investors because it may contain many concessions made to rent seeking groups. Institutional rules, however, may play an important role in mediating the dispute. Although none of the cases in the study had this outcome, the case of Puerto Rico may be a good example. Buyers considered the selling price to be too expensive, and hence the company was not sold.

CONCEPTUAL ORGANIZATION

The analysis is conducted in six chapters. This first chapter introduces the central literature and arguments. It then suggests an alternative argument and lays out the theoretical framework. The next four chapters explore the microeconomic, macroeconomic, and political factors that affected the divestiture of state-owned telecommunications companies in the four countries of the Southern Cone of Latin America. A single chapter is dedicated to each case. Chapter 2 examines Brazil; chapter 3, Chile; chapter 4, Uruguay; and chapter 5, Argentina. Each chapter begins with an examination of the privatization attempt. Each case is subsequently dissected to gain maximum insight into the various factors that affected the privatization. The sections on microeconomic factors focus on the economic history of each company. They examine the industries' early history and microeconomic development. For example, factors such as long-distance/urban networks and technology are studied. They also analyze the impact of the microeconomic structure on performance and on rent seeking groups. The sections on macroeconomic factors focuses on the impact of macroeconomic events on the development of each SOE. The emphasis is on the impact of fiscal policies, inflation, debt, and multilateral agency policies. The third sections examine the effect of the political environment on the privatization process. Since these cases occur in newly democratized countries, each section begins with an analysis of the transition to democracy in order to assess the absolute and relative powers of the national executive. It moves to an examination of the key interest groups involved in the sale of the telephone company, and their formal and informal organizational capacities to shape the privatization process. Last, the political section studies the institutional rules and organizations that impact the privatization process.

In the course of the discussion, the political section focuses on the absolute and relative strengths of the government and the interest groups, along with their political strategies. The sixth, and last, chapter ties together the analyses and suggests conclusions. It also provides a statistical analysis of the three general sets of questions. The latter examines the microeconomic, macroeconomic, and political data with a battery of univariate tests to investigate the variation in the outcome. In order to increase the comparative power of the analysis, the data set consists of the attempts to privatize the telecommunication companies in twenty-two developed and developing countries (Table 5).[20] There are two goals for this analysis. The first is to test the generalizations made by the four case studies. The second is to measure the correlation between the variables.

Table 5
Attempts to Privatize State Telecommunication Companies in 22 Developed and Developing Countries

Developed	Countries	Developing	Countries
Accepted	Rejected	Accepted	Rejected
Great Britain	Greece	Argentina '90	Argentina '88
New Zealand		Malaysia	Uruguay
Japan		Jamaica	Colombia
Czech Republic		Mexico*	Thailand
Hungary		Chile	Brazil
		Peru	South Africa
		Pakistan	India
		Singapore	
		Panama	
		Bolivia	

*In 1994, Mexico became a member of the OECD, but it was not a member at the time of the privatization attempt.

The case material shows that the microeconomic factors had a minimal impact on the privatization process. In other words, company performance had only a marginal impact on whether a telephone company would be privatized. All of the countries, however, considered privatization options when they entered into a macroeconomic crisis. The Brazilian experience with high inflation driven by huge fiscal deficits forced the government to consider privatization; however, it could not get the program implemented. The Chilean government did not consider privatization of the large SOEs until after the financial crisis of 1982. Uruguay faced distortions in the fiscal situation; nonetheless, the economy was relatively sound. Hence, there was no pressing drive to privatize the telephone company. Argentina, however, faced a dire economic situation during its first attempt to sell ENTEL, but conditions deteriorated to national emergency proportions and the new Menem government was forced to reconsider selling the company.

NOTES

1. Most privatization programs have involved sectors with monopoly characteristics. Hence, privatization of sectors with monopoly characteristics has been the most controversial because they had the potential to move monopoly rents between political groups (Glade, 1989).

2. The case studies go through 1995. Subsequent cases were not used at the time of this writing.

3. In 1991, global telecommunications accounted for approximately $540 billion or 20% of the global GDP. It is also usually the largest employer in developing countries and accounts for 5—10% of developing countries GDP (Institutional Investor, 1992).

4. Although I assume that the government will attempt to maximize price, I recognize that many governments may have to forgo a higher selling price in order to gain a quick sale. A reduction in price in order to facilitate the divestiture, however, may represent an important economic benefit to the country because opening access to capital inflow is an important consideration for governments faced with financial crises.

5. Argentina is the core case in the research project. The Argentine government made two attempts to privatize its state-owned telecommunications company. The first attempt was rejected by the Argentine Congress and was a factor in the collapse of the administration. The second attempt was initiated by the opposition party, which had led the fight against the first attempt. The sale was executed during this attempt. The purpose of focusing on Argentina is to control for exogenous variables that otherwise complicate the comparison.

6. A divestiture is marked by a change in the company's ownership title and is recorded in the company financial records.

7. Most of the case material was based on extensive interviews with telecommunications experts, government ministers, and executives in the Southern Cone. Explicit reference to the interview material is not made since many individuals spoke on a confidential basis. The interviews were conducted from January 1993 to June 1993 during a field research project that was supported by the Ford Foundation.

8. The following should be noted. First, since the cases in my research involved international investment banks, which issued shares on global markets, the transfer date will also be recorded in public documents such as stock prospectus. Second, the dependent variable in this analysis is the divestiture of state-owned telephone companies.

9. The term "microeconomic" refers to company-level factors, as opposed to macroeconomic factors, which refer to country-level factors.

10. Given the important role of the general population in the Schattschneider framework, firm performance can provide important insight into how the general population perceives the telephone company. Therefore, another way of seeing microeconomic efficiency is that it can serve as a proxy for consumer sentiment. Nonetheless,

it is important to note that this is not a perfect proxy. Due to the low level of telephone communications in developing countries, not all citizens have access to telephone lines. Hence, they are liable to be swayed by other forces, such as media campaigns and nationalistic feelings about transferring a national asset to a foreign owner.

11. The telecommunications industry has established several standards to measure telephone performance. These statistics are issued by every telephone company and are maintained by the International Telephone Union, an agency of the United Nations, in Switzerland. The three major standards are line density, employees per line, and investment per line.

12. The role of conditionality in policy-making decisions has been the subject of intense research by Kahler (1989) and Fishlow (1991).

13. The literature on rent-seeking (Krueger, 1974) argued that the manipulation of markets by political arrangements created rents for privileged groups. These rents, often highly distortionary, were vehemently defended by the groups involved.

14. It is important to note that the power of the president is important in more than securing approval for the privatization program. It is also important in altering the rent seeking structure of state firms so that they can become attractive to international investors.

15. This argument is in line with Cook and Minogue's (1990) finding that the ability to implement economic reform programs—such as privatization—in developing countries is largely determined by the political resources available to the group pushing for the reforms.

16. Williamson (1994) suggests that the honeymoon period is based on the hypothesis that extensive reforms have to be implemented immediately after a government takes office.

17. Schneider's (1992) analysis of privatization also was based on a variation of the collective action problem. He concluded that the compensation of central interest groups in return for their cooperation could exceed the political and economic resources available to the national executive. Therefore, the executive must play a very well-orchestrated coordination game to control the payoffs to key interest groups.

18. Schattschneider (1960) suggested that the expansion of the conflict beyond the control of any of the parties resulted in a situation where any outcome was possible. Nonetheless, the loss of control of an economic program probably will result not in a random outcome but in defeat of the proposition.

19. Geddes (1994) argued that institutions either mute or magnify the effects of interest group pressure on government decision makers.

20. While there are many criteria for developed and developing countries, I categorize developed countries as those that belonged to the OECD during the privatization attempt. I categorize all others as developing.

2

BRAZIL

OVERVIEW

Privatization has been a topic of intense discussion and debate in Brazil since the early 1980s. The first privatization program was launched in 1979, with the creation of the National Debureaucratization Program and the Special State Enterprise Secretariat. In 1981, this was followed by the Special Privatization Commission. While both programs failed to implement any divestitures, the inauguration of President José Sarney five years later promised to re-invigorate the process. This, however, did not turn out to be the case, since only a few symbolic divestitures were made. In total, 38 SOEs were sold from 1981 to 1989.

As the end of the 1980s approached, however, pressure to increase the pace of privatization in Brazil grew. On March 15, 1990, Fernando Collor de Mello, of the PDS party, was elected president. The 39-year-old governor of the tiny and impoverished state of Alagoas inherited a country with monthly inflation of 84% and a bloated public sector consisting of 200 state-owned enterprises (SOEs) that had a combined deficit of $60 billion. His campaign platform consisted of economic and political reforms designed to restructure and improve the economy. Collor targeted the "maharajas"—the unproductive, highly paid, and politically well-connected bureaucrats on the government payroll—as a principal cause of Brazil's economic problems (R. Nelson, 1994).

He vowed to sweep out corruption and inflation by shrinking the state, selling public companies, and reducing import barriers. He abolished 11 state firms and 13 agencies, dismissed 7,000 personnel, and promised to privatize an SOE every month. Unfortunately, the attempt to privatize the Brazilian telephone company was a short-lived initiative.

In 1991, President Collor revived the privatization initiative by creating the National Destatization Program (PND). This program differed from the earlier attempts by identifying specific target companies for divestiture, establishing a master privatization schedule, and allowing foreign participation (BNDES, 1992). The program was successful in privatizing 26 small and medium-sized SOEs, but it was unable to sell off the larger strategic companies, such as Telebras, Petrobras, CVRD, and Electrobras. In early 1991, the president sent a constitutional amendment to the Brazilian Congress to allow private sector operations in telecommunications.

The constitutional prohibition against the privatization of the telephone company was linked to Brazil's return to democratic rule in 1984. The departure of the military brought a wave of democratic euphoria, and a new Constitutional Assembly was formed (1987–1988) to draft a document that provided political and economic guarantees for Brazilians; however, the new document had very precise rules that constrained the economy. The 1988 Constitution declared that the energy and telecommunications sectors were strategic industries and could not be privately owned. Therefore, any attempt by the Collor administration to privatize the telephone company necessitated a constitutional amendment, a measure that required an affirmative vote by 70% of both congressional houses. The administration, however, lacked the political support to make such changes.

Faced with an aborted privatization attempt in 1991, the government took unilateral actions to liberalize the telecommunications sector and increase foreign participation in the industry. Infrastructure Minister Ozires Silva introduced a package of 10 government rules to open the sector to private Brazilian and foreign companies. They were allowed to begin operating mobile telephone and satellite communications, areas hitherto reserved for the state telecommunications company, Telebras. By allowing greater levels of competition, the liberalization of the telecommunications sector was considered a first step to privatization.[1] However, unions, SOE managers, and industry leaders mobilized and lobbied the Congress to oppose the liberalization. By the end of 1991, further attempts to restructure the telecommunications industry by Economy Minister Zelia Cardoso de Mello were flatly rejected by the Congress, and the program was placed on indefinite hold.

MICROECONOMIC FACTORS

Formation and Early History

The first Brazilian telegraph line was installed in Rio de Janeiro on May 11, 1852. The communications network grew steadily, and by 1857, there were 50 kilometers of lines between the capital (Rio de Janeiro) and Petrópolis. Telegraph communications later surged during the War of the Triple Alliance (1865–1870) against Paraguay. In order to improve communications with field commanders, the government expanded the telegraph network to the north and west.

Telephone service arrived in Brazil in 1876, after Emperor Pedro II visited an exposition in Philadelphia at which Alexander Graham Bell was demonstrating his new invention, the telephone. The Brazilian emperor, a technology aficionado, immediately ordered the first telephone line for Brazil, which was installed in his palace. The first large telephone network was established on November 15, 1879, when Charles Paul Mackie obtained a concession to provide service between Rio de Janeiro and the suburb of Niterói. The firm consisted of U.S. investors and was called the Telephone Company of Brazil. While foreign-owned telephone companies spread to other urban areas, Brazilian businessmen led the expansion of telephone networks into the interior of the country. In 1881, the emperor granted Carlos Monteiro e Souza permission to provide telephone service in the province of Pará. As telephone use increased, the government granted individual states and municipalities control of telephone concessions. In 1890, however, the Brazilian government reversed itself and established a national agency to grant concessions.

Development of the industry came to a standstill with the end of the monarchy and the start of World War I. The departure of the emperor removed a strong ally and guiding force for the industry, and the war broke off access to North American and European technology and equipment. Hence, the network entered a prolonged period of decay, and expansion of the system did not resume until 1922. In the 1930s, however, the Brazilian network again experienced a dramatic rate of growth. For example, the Rio de Janeiro network surged to over 99,000 lines. But investment and development came to a grinding halt in the 1940s as the world entered a second global war. Brazilian firms again could not obtain new equipment or essential replacement parts, pushing the system back into decay.

Up to this point, control of the larger firms remained mostly in the hands of foreign investors. German and Canadian multinationals now owned and operated the major urban telephone concessions. Government intervention was minimal and the industry was mostly self-regulated. Telephone firms negotiated tariffs with each other and final approval was given by the government. In the 1950s, however, the government began to increase its level of intervention as the Brazilian state began to play a more interventionist role in the private sector (R. Nelson, 1994). Increases in telephone rates were delayed or very small increases were authorized. Private companies became concerned at the growing government activity in the industry, and in 1960 they started reducing their level of investment, thus plunging the Brazilian telecommunications sector into a third period of contraction. Hence, the history of the Brazilian network has been characterized by spasmodic cycles of expansion followed by periods of contraction and decay.

Political Influence and Control

In 1960, there were over 1,000 telephone companies and concessions operating in Brazil. The multiplicity of firms led to a wide array of technologies and a high level of incompatibility between systems. There also were few long-distance lines and no central planning. To increase coordination between the different telephone companies and systems, the government decided to take a role that was more pro-active than rate-setting. On March 31, 1962, the Brazilian government passed legislation that instituted uniform tariffs, provided for new investment, and assured telephone service in vital areas of the economy, such as banking and manufacturing (Telebras, 1977). In 1965, the government took a radical step and entered the telecommunications market as a competitor.[2] It formed a new telecommunications SOE, Embratel, to provide long distance telephone service.

Private companies provided extensive telephone services in urban regions, large cities, and municipalities, where there were large concentrations of customers. In contrast, they provided very little long-distance service. Not only did long-distance service require expensive equipment and investment, but also required moving into and across the territories of other telephone companies, resulting in a complicated coordination problem. The state development agencies, however, perceived the absence of a national telecommunication network as a major obstacle to economic integration and development. Armed with the power of eminent domain and large resources, the government decided that it was the only economic actor capable of resolving the long-distance communications problem (Telebras, 1977).

Investments in the new network were financed with government funds and through a 30% surcharge on all telephone rates. In 1966, the government decided to continue its expansion into the rest of the telecommunications sector and authorized Embratel to acquire a majority share in Companhia Telefónica Brasileira (CTB). CTB was a subsidiary of the Canadian-owned Brazilian Traction Light & Power and the largest telephone company in Brazil. With the acquisition of CTB, Embratel gained control of the six largest telephone operations in Brazil, including São Paulo, Minas Gerais, and Espírito Santo. Nonetheless, there still remained almost 1,000 small operators that provided services to small villages, towns, and rural regions. Therefore, in 1972, the government decided to create a federal holding company that would integrate all of Brazil's regions under a single public owner and technological format while providing a uniform plan of investment. The new company, called Telebras, was divided into 30 regional subsidiaries or units. Telebras was also given control of Embratel, raising the number of subsidiaries to 31 (see Table 6).

Table 6
Telecommunication Units of Telebras

Bambui	Teleron	Telamazon	Teleacre	Telaima
Telepara	Telma	Telepisa	Teleceara	Telern
Telpa	Telpe	Telasa	Telergipe	Telebahia
Telemig	Telest	Telerj	Cetel	Telebrasilia
Telegoias	Telemat	Telesp	Telespar	Telesc
CRT	CTBC	CTMR	Cotelpa	Teleamapa
Embratel				

Source: Telebras, 1990.

The holding company structure allowed telephone operations to be decentralized, with most operating decisions delegated to the local level. Dmytraczenko (1993) argued that Telebras was designed to minimize political meddling by creating a buffer between the political leadership located in Brasília and the managers for the individual companies in the group. The Ministry of Communications in Brasilia had general responsibility of the firm, but local managers were able to operate in a manner that allowed them to maximize efficiency while enjoying many of the benefits and resources of centralized technology and investment. In other words, the individual units were allowed to operate as if they were private companies. There was very little actual regulation, and ministries rarely interfered with company affairs. Nonetheless, at the local level, there was significant political control over employment issues. Many politicians allocated positions in Telebras operating units as political patronage. Company employees were considered public-sector employees, making them eligible for public sector wages and constitutional guarantees. Therefore, the holding company was relatively independent at a national level, but the local operating units had a fairly high level of political interference.

Firm Performance

Telebras' performance was mixed. In absolute terms it performed very well, while on a comparative basis it was not very strong. The Brazilian telephone company posted record rates of growth during its early history. In the first year of operation, it had only 2 million telephone lines; however, by the mid-1970s it was one of the 15 largest telephone networks in the world. Annual long-distance calls increased from 3 million in 1969 to more than 450 million in 1987, and telex subscribers increased from 2,000 to 93,000 during the same period.   But in relative terms, the company appeared to perform poorly. Part of this was due to the size and dispersion of the Brazilian population. Faced with a population of 90 million at the outset, and a strong population growth rate, Telebras could hardly expand fast enough to improve telephone density ratios. Furthermore, the country had an imbalance between population concentration and economic activity. Most of Brazil's population is concentrated in the northeastern section of the country, yet 80% of GDP is produced in the southeastern section of the country. Furthermore, about 46 million people, one-third of the total population, are located in the rural interior sections. These rural areas encompass 4,200 small cities and 4,300 towns—70 percent of which have fewer than 2,500 people. Given such an uneven dispersal of the population, the company was hampered in its expansion of the telephone network.

Often the rural and poor regions were left with outdated and poorly performing technology while the more populous and economically important areas received new and expensive technology. Nonetheless, a telephone system is akin to a chain. That is, the system is only as strong as its weakest link. Often breakdowns in the overall telephone system could be traced to problems in areas with older technology. Therefore, on a comparative basis, Telebras' performance was not impressive. Table 7 shows that in absolute terms, Telebras was the largest of the four telephone networks in the Southern Cone, but in comparative terms, it rated third out of the four cases in the number of lines per 100 inhabitants and second in revenues collected per line.

Table 7
Comparative Performance Statistics, 1986–1991

	1986	1987	1988	1989	1990	1991
Argentina						
Lines/100	9.30	8.71	10.07	10.65	10.8	12.1
Telephone Lines	2,859,209	2,711,973	3,175,756	3,400,000	3,481,195	3,718,508
Revenue per Line	$1,124	$549	$604	$555	$571	$745
Brazil						
Lines/100	8.27	8.49	8.8	8.74	8.9	9.2
Telephone Lines	6,835,000	7,155,000	7,584,000	8,041,000	8,536,000	10,075,324
Revenue per Line	$366	$431	$541	$647	$670	$590
Chile						
Lines/100	4.53	4.63	4.91	4.98	6.16	9.2
Telephone Lines	557,987	580,795	625,466	645,863	722,458	997,000
Revenue per Line	$486	$518	$589	$869	$670	$540
Uruguay						
Lines/100	10.15	10.26	11.29	12.21	13.4	14.0
Telephone Lines	306,926	311,984	345,390	375,830	415,403	451,000
Revenue per Line	$427	$332	$353	$416	$463	$468

Sources: ITU, 1992; Booz Allen & Hamilton, 1991; Salomon Brothers, 1993

Technology

The development of Brazil's technology base was one of the driving forces behind the government investment program in Telebras. The experience of the two world wars encouraged Brazilian planners to create a viable domestic telecommunications industry. Government officials argued that a self-sufficient Brazilian technological base would help suppress the spasmodic cycles of growth and decay that had characterized Brazilian development during the first half of the twentieth century.

Technology transfer from industrialized countries to Brazil, however, was a tricky issue. The telecommunication companies in the industrialized nations jealously protected their technology. They, along with other technology-intensive industries, would not agree to wholesale technology transfer, but agreed to locate equipment assembly plants in Brazil. Development officials accepted to the proposal, and reasoning that even if the new telephone assembly plants involved very few technology intensive processes, the mere location of the plants on Brazilian soil would produce positive spillover effects (Evans, 1979). The construction of the domestic telecommunications industrial base was accelerated in 1974, after the severe shock of the oil crisis and the surge in commodity prices. Brazil's complete dependence on foreign oil and its high energy costs absorbed much of its foreign exchange. Ironically, the government immediately began exploring ways of reducing nonoil import costs through import-substitution programs. In 1974, it established Grupo Executivo Interministerial de Componentes e Materiales (GEICOM) to lead the task. GEICOM identified telecommunications equipment as a good candidate for import substitution, and in the 1976 the government established the national telecommunications research and manufacturing complex, Centro de Pesquisa e Desenvolvimento (CPqD), in Campinas, a city outside São Paulo.

CPqD telephone labs were the most advanced outside the industrialized world, and the only ones of their kind in Latin America. Bell Labs in the United States and the Alcatel labs in France set the standard for telecommunications technology in the industrialized world, and CPqD was chartered to do the same for Brazil. The unit not only refined and improved Telebras' standard electromechanical equipment, it also spearheaded the country's push into microelectronic technology (Hobday, 1990). Nonetheless, the Brazilian effort was dwarfed by the R&D spending in the United States and Europe. In 1991, Telebras funneled about $2.4 billion in scarce resources to establish a Brazilian technical telephone standard, whereas the U.S., Japanese, and European laboratories spent 4 to 5 times more (CS First Boston, 1994b).

The CPqD complex designed an indigenous telephone system called Tropico. Tropico was, and continues to be, a viable system that uses digital, satellite, and fiber-optic technology, but it has a high level of incompatibility with the telephone systems used in the rest of the world. The divergence between Tropico and international standards has increased, thus isolating Brazil from the rest of the world. Telebras also has been left with the high costs of performing original research that has already been done by the major telephone laboratories, thus forcing it to reinvent the wheel again and again. This is an expensive proposition for a company and country that operate on relatively few resources. With the oil crisis over and oil prices at historical lows, Brazil has been left with the heavy burden of continued funding of the Tropico system. Political considerations, such as national pride and employment, and the logic of sunk costs, however, prevent Brazil from returning to international technology. In other words, it had begun to follow a very path dependent pattern of development (Haggard and Kaufman, 1992b).

It is very difficult to gauge a company's level of technological development; however, Beca (1991) suggested using the level of digitalization as a proxy. Table 8 underscores Brazil's low rate of digitalization compared with the rest of the Southern Cone. It is clear that Brazil's digitalization program lagged that of its neighbors by four to five years.

Table 8
Digitalization Statistics for Southern Cone, 1986–1991

	1986	1987	1988	1989	1990	1991
Chile	36.8	36.0	37.9	36.0	64.0	71.0
Uruguay	2.0	17.0	33.0	53.0	58.0	63.0
Brazil	0.9	2.8	6.0	10.3	13.7	16.0
Argentina	0	0	9.1	11.1	13.8	17.0

Sources: CTC, 1990; Salomon Brothers, 1993; ANTEL, 1992; ITU, 1992

Investment and Financing

Like many telephone companies in the region, Telebras used self-financing for funding its expansion programs. This meant the use of internal resources, such as tariff rates and installation fees, to purchase new equipment, perform research and development (R&D), manage the operating system, and expand the network. In 1972, the government created the Fondo Nacional de Telecomunicaciones (FNT) to pool Telebras internal assets for equal disbursement throughout the entire Telebras system. In the 1980s, however, the FNT funds were depleted and the company had to look elsewhere for capital.

Telebras and its subsidiaries shifted their focus from internal sources to domestic and international capital markets. Because of the large size of its revenue base and assets, the company was able to tap into both the Brazilian capital markets, and the international ones. On several occasions the company floated bonds in the international capital markets, a feat that none of the other state-owned Latin American phone companies was able to achieve. The ownership structure also was altered to allow minority equity participation by private investors, with control remaining in the hands of the state. Telebras and the subsidiaries for São Paulo and Rio de Janeiro, Telesp and Telerj, used the São Paulo stock market (Bovespa) to float shares. The company's total investment dwarfed those of the other Latin American counties (see Table 9) and its rate of return was also good—10% for 1988 and 6% for 1989, the year prior to the attempted privatization. In investment per line, Brazil ranked third out of the four countries in the Southern Cone (see Table 9). As in the other categories, the company's financial condition was not very good.

Table 9
Investment in the Telecommunications Sector, 1986–1991

	1986	1987	1988	1989	1990	1991
Chile						
Total Investment (million $)	187	191	245	488	532	372
Investment /Line	235	234	430	794	845	345
Uruguay						
Total Investment (million $)	70	71	68	56	48	59
Investment/Line	240	227	198	151	116	130
Brazil						
Total Investment (Millions $)	1,245	1,447	1,870	2,059	2,226	2,448
Investment/Line	94	104	133	145	173	175
Argentina						
Total Investment (million $)	291	546	1,086	457	232	301
Investment/Line	102	187	332	132	66	75

Sources: Wajnberg, 1990; ITU 1992; Salomon Brothers, 1993.

Equipment Manufacturing and Purchasing

Prior to the establishment of the CPqD laboratories and equipment manufacturing plants, the Brazilian government created incentives for foreign companies to establish facilities within the country. This was part of the general imports substitution industrialization (ISI) strategy the country was pursuing. The first manufacturing operations were established in the 1950s for the production of transmission equipment. Soon European, Japanese, and North American firms, such as Standard Electric-ITT, Ericsson, Nippon Electric, and Siemens, built large equipment plants. The facilities, however, tended to be assembly plants. Much of the equipment was designed and manufactured abroad, then shipped to Brazil for final assembly (Wajnberg, 1990). Hence, while there was some technology transfer, it was limited in scope.

As the CPqD facilities matured during the late 1970s and early 1980s, the government began to require that equipment manufacturers perform a larger part of their technology-intensive manufacturing process in Brazil. General Jose Antonio Alencastro e Silva, the head of Telebras during the late 1970s, sought to create spillover effects, such as technician training and subcontracting activities, that would have a greater impact on Brazil's technological base (*Latin American Newsletter*, 1978). In return, multinational corporations were granted exclusive rights to markets and higher returns (Evans, 1979).

One of the results of this policy was the creation of large and powerful economic interest groups. Since manufacturers of domestic telephone equipment had a captive client in Telebras and the country had cut itself off from trade competition through import substitution, the manufacturers sold telephone equipment to Telebras at prices that were higher than international rates. A domestic lobby was spawned with the high rents from these exclusive markets and soon became a powerful force against privatization. Not only did the privatization of Telebras mean increased competition from external sources for equipment and a reduction in rents, it also implied the transformation of the Tropico technology to international standards. Therefore, the manufacturers would have to make large investments to retool their industry to meet international standards.

Labor

The Brazilian labor movement experienced a strong revival during the mid-1980s. The return to democratic rule and the decline of military repression allowed labor organizations to band together into peak-level associations (Helena and Alves, 1989). While the number of groups multiplied, three unions emerged in the late 1980s as the most powerful peak associations: Central Unica dos Trabalhadores (CUT), Forca Sindical (FS), and Confederaçao Geral dos Trabalhadores (CGT) (Langevin, 1994). The CUT stood out as the most militant and left-of-center association; the CGT adopted a more centrist position; and the FS became a progressive union of high-technology workers. Pent-up worker's demands and frustration from the days of the military dictatorship produced higher levels of militancy and strikes. Workers banded together to form political parties that played central roles in the writing of the 1988 Constitution.

Through congressional seats held by the CUT's political party, Partido dos Trabalhadores (PT), and an intensive lobbying campaign by most organized labor groups, the unions were able to secure key clauses in the Constitution affecting the privatization of the largest SOEs and worker's rights. Telecommunications and energy were declared strategic sectors, and the government was unable to privatize state companies in those sectors without a constitutional amendment—a politically expensive proposition. Workers also were constitutionally mandated generous benefits. Workers in SOEs were granted 2 months' severance pay for every year of employment, plus five months' wages (Jatoba, 1994). Given the political manipulations at the local level, Telebras became a bloated enterprise with too many employees. Although its use of labor was more efficient in 1986–1987, it failed to keep up with the efficiency gains made by many of the other Southern Cone telephone companies (see Table 10).

Table 10
Comparative Labor Efficiency, 1986–1992

	1986	1987	1988	1989	1990	1991	1992
Chile: CTC							
Gross Revenue per Employee	24,756	26,689	45,942	56,289	59,265	67,370	80,984
Lines Per Employee	72.8	72.5	78.0	87.0	93.0	125.0	151.0
Brazil: Telebras							
Gross Revenue per Employee	25,758	31,367	41,873	52,911	49,316	49,242	65,994
Lines Per Employee	25.7	31.3	41.8	52.9	49.3	49.2	55.0
Uruguay: ANTEL							
Gross Revenue per Employee	9,032	9,502	8,664	8,497	8,133	7,541	7,355
Lines per Employee	38.0	37.0	39.8	44.2	51.7	59.8	66.1
Argentina: Entel							
Gross Revenue per Employee	69,469	31,761	40,936	40,986	46,685	57,992	76,047
Lines Per Employee	62.3	57.9	67.4	73.2	81.7	102.0	105.0

Sources: Salomon Brothers, 1993; ITU, 1992; CTC, 1990; ANTEL, 1992.

MACROECONOMIC FACTORS

This section analyzes Brazil's macroeconomic factors to search for explanations behind the aborted divestiture of Telebras. According to the literature examined Chapter 1, privatization becomes more likely when countries face macroeconomic crises. This section employs a framework that examines the impact of fiscal performance, inflation, foreign debt, and growth (GDP) on the privatization initiative. It also explores the influence that multilateral lending agencies had on macroeconomic policies, especially as they impacted the process of macroeconomic structural adjustment and privatization.

Fiscal Performance and Inflation

Like most of the countries in the Southern Cone, Brazil entered the twentieth century with an agenda to transform itself from an underdeveloped country into a developed one (Evans, 1979). Most economists and policy makers attributed the low level of Brazilian development to a failure of market forces and the absence of domestic entrepreneurs with significant levels of capital. Nonetheless, since Brazil is a country rich in minerals, land, and commodities, the national leadership decided to undertake a massive state-led industrialization program. In the 1930s, President Getúlio Vargas initiated an epoch of state building by which the government significantly enlarged its role as the primary stimulus and guide of economic development. This process was accelerated during the postwar period by President Juscelino Kubitschek (Skidmore, 1967). Because the country lacked sophisticated financial resources, especially long-term financial credits, to fund such a massive investment program, it delegated a much larger role to the state.[3] Brazil's new economic model allowed the state to alleviate the development bottleneck by expanding the country's industrial base.

At the heart of the development program was the National Development Bank (BNDES), established in 1952 to finance both private and public industrialization efforts. BNDES resolved the country's long-term financial problems by offering long-term loans (ten to fifteen years) and credits, performing this task by using both public funds and foreign debt. The new development program led by BNDES produced excellent results and soon was widely accepted by the country's political and economic actors. Despite two severe oil crises during the 1970s, Brazilian GDP grew 158% in real terms during the decade; the highest rate of inflation was in 1979, reaching 77.2%. This period is now known as the Brazilian miracle. The dramatic expansion of the economy was driven by domestic demand, particularly for durable consumer goods, and was aided by financial support for industrial development. With the level of investment reaching almost 25% of GDP during the decade, Brazil was able to develop strong capacities in engineering and chemical products (*Euromoney*, 1994).

The experiences of the 1970s allowed Brazil to develop a general consensus on a short list of national priorities. At the top of the list was economic growth, followed by export performance, and at the end was economic stability or inflation. In other words, political and economic forces allowed the government to operate with high fiscal deficits as long as the economy was continuing to grow and export earnings were high—despite the fact that the fiscal disequilibrium that was driving much of this growth was also producing high rates of inflation (Lal and Maxfield, 1993).

The unchecked growth of the economy, however, eventually created strains. By 1976, oil comprised almost 31% of total imports, or $3.8 billion, and the servicing of its energy requirements sapped the investment capacity of the state. By the end of the 1980s, GDP growth slowed to 33.5% for the decade, while the annual inflation registered 1,765%.

The driving force behind the escalating fiscal deficit and mounting inflation was the huge and inefficient state sector. In the 1970s, state-owned companies expanded at an exponential rate; from 1966 to 1977, 219 SOEs were established (Pinheiro and Schneider, 1993). Although the program greatly expanded the industrial base, few of the larger companies became profitable. In 1987, the 513 state-owned companies generated an estimated loss of $4 billion. Most of the shortfall was produced by a handful of state enterprises that controlled essential sectors of the economy. Among them were Electrobras, the electricity monopoly; Siderbras, the steel corporation; R.F.F.S.A., the railroad company, and Nuclearbras, the nuclear energy entity. The latter spent $5 billion on a reactor that was rarely operational. But not all SOE operations generated losses. Petrobras, the oil SOE, showed a profit almost every year it was in operation. The state mining corporation, Vale do Rio Doce (CVRD), and the aircraft manufacturer, Embraer, were profitable and produced strong export earnings. As Table 11 illustrates, many of the large state owned companies nonetheless produced large losses. Table 12 shows that they all absorbed very high levels of capital.

Table 11
SOE Performance in 1988

Company	Sector	1988 Sales in billions $	Earnings in millions $
Petrobras	Oil	$18.5	$1,274.5
Telebras	Telephones	3.6	469.5
CVRD	Mining	2.3	129.7
Electrobras	Electricity	10.0	(875.9)
Siderbras	Steel	6.8	(641.2)
Itaipu	Electricity	1.9	(632.4)
Nuclearbras	Nuclear energy	1.5	(616.5)
R.F.F.S.A.	Railroads	1.9	(512.9)

Source: Brazilian Planning Ministry.

Table 12
SOE Investment, 1989 and 1990 (billions U.S. $)

Group	Sector	1989	1990
Electrobras	Energy	2.74	3.17
Petrobras	Petroleum	2.71	3.17
Telebras	Communications	1.95	2.81
CVRD	Mining	0.47	0.83
R.F.F.S.A.	Railways	0.47	0.28
Siderbras	Steel	0.62	0.67

Source: Brazilian Planning Ministry.

State ownership of Telebras especially strained Brazil's resources. The company's capitalization and expansion programs forced the government to allocate capital that would have otherwise been slated for social programs and for other crucial infrastructure projects. Furthermore, as Brazil's economy deteriorated during the late 1980s, the government was forced to abandon many crucial network maintenance programs. The national treasury transformed the telecommunications sector into a source of fiscal funding by piggybacking special taxes onto telephone bills and appropriating most of the Telebras surplus (*The Economist*, 1986). Last of all, the ever-increasing level of inflation seriously undermined the strength of the telephone company by effectively reducing the prices of telecommunications services in real terms, thus decreasing whatever investment capital remained available for expansion (*Business Latin America*, 1993a).

In 1986, Brazil launched a series of stabilization moves to bring the macroeconomic situation under control. The Cruzado Stabilization Plan instituted a new currency (the cruzado) and froze prices. Although the inflation rate declined to 65% year-over-year, an unprecedented consumer boom, due to the new stability in prices and wage hikes, destroyed the plan. The Cruzado Plan was followed by a series of other stabilization plans that included, the Cruzado II Plan in November 1986, the Bresser Plan in June 1987, the Summer Plan in January 1989, and the Collor Plan in 1990. All of the plans were successful in reducing inflation for several months, but they all eventually failed due to the inability of the government to control its fiscal situation. As Table 13 indicates, Brazil's fiscal deficit was the largest in the Southern Cone, and by most standards, it was one of the largest in the world. This deficit fueled the country's high rate of inflation, and even pushed Brazil into hyperinflation in 1990 (see Table 14).

Table 13
Fiscal Balance in the Southern Cone Countries, 1985–1992 (% of GDP)

	1985	1986	1987	1988	1989	1990	1991	1992
Brazil	-19.2	-8.9	17.8	-28.2	-51.0	-11.5	-6.4	-45.0
Argentina	-2.6	-2.0	-6.5	-7.0	-21.8	-3.3	-1.8	0.8
Chile	-6.9	-3.3	-0.2	-2.0	2.4	1.0	1.6	0.5
Uruguay	-3.1	-1.3	-1.3	-2.0	-3.4	-5.0	0.4	0.3

Source: International Institute of Finance, 1992–1994

Table 14
CPI Inflation Rates in the Southern Cone, 1985–1992 (Average % change)

	1985	1986	1987	1988	1989	1990	1991	1992
Brazil	238	141	230	638	1,475	2,864	434	1,129
Argentina	618	75	131	343	3,079	2,314	171	17
Chile	32	19	21	12	21	27	18	12
Uruguay	74	71	63	62	81	112	102	58

Source: International Institute of Finance, 1992-1994

Faced with an overwhelming fiscal burden, the Brazilian leadership pondered two choices of what to do with its SOEs: privatize or restructure? The government chose the latter. Rather than pursuing privatization as an option to reduce the fiscal burden, the government worked on reducing the deficit of each SOE. Unfortunately, this strategy forced even greater levels of decay on the telephone network because the government limited company investment, maintenance, and imports. Thus, in a perverse way, the government's decisions to improve SOE operations paved the way for more inefficiency.

Another important macroeconomic factor is the role of GDP growth. Although most theorists have failed to consider the impact of growth on privatization, it may actually be an important macroeconomic factor. Countries experiencing high inflation rates and poor fiscal performances usually experience patterns of low growth, but this may not always be the case. Some governments may actually use fiscal resources to artificially stimulate growth, and this may reduce some of the pressures to divest state-owned assets. This clearly was the case in Brazil during the 1980s. As has been suggested earlier, Brazil had a consensus on high inflation rates in return for strong growth. Table 15 shows that the country, indeed, produced strong growth from 1985 to 1989, but the pattern changed after 1989. During 1991 and 1992, the time-period of the privatization attempt of Telebras, Brazilian economic performance was very poor. Hence, negative growth may have had very little effect on the country's decision to privatize.

Table 15
GDP Growth in the Southern Cone, 1985–1992

Country	1985	1986	1987	1988	1989	1990	1991	1992
Brazil	5.8	7.6	3.6	-0.1	3.3	-4.0	1.1	-0.9
Argentina	-6.6	5.6	2.3	-5.1	-4.6	0.4	6.0	8.7
Chile	2.4	5.7	5.7	7.4	10.0	2.1	6.0	10.3
Uruguay	1.5	8.9	7.9	0	1.3	0.9	2.9	7.7

Source: International Institute of Finance, 1992–1994.

Foreign Debt

In addition to fiscal deficits, the financing for the ambitious Brazilian industrialization drive during the 1960s and 1970s was built on the backs of huge trade deficits and foreign debts. During the period from 1950 to 1986, Brazil had a surplus in its balance of payments in only 8 years. With more inflows than outflows, the country often faced difficulties in servicing its debt. In 1964, Brazil was forced to reschedule its foreign obligations following a military coup, yet the international financial community remained unconcerned about its large current account deficit or the growing size of the total debt (Cardoso and Dornbusch, 1991). It was not until Mexico defaulted on its debt in 1982 that the international financial community began to regard Brazil as a credit risk. Soon, most sources of new funds were eliminated and Brazil was unable to rollover existing short-term credits. Furthermore, the need to service the ever-growing energy requirements (and the explosion of energy prices) placed Brazil in a precarious situation. Faced with a downturn in the global economy and depressed export prices, Brazil was placed under even tighter constraints.[4]

With its back against the wall, Brazil declared a moratorium on all debt service in 1986 and officially isolated itself from the international financial community. The economic leadership shifted its focus from the development of internal markets to export promotion in an attempt to improve its external situation. Although the new measures allowed Brazil to post surpluses in its current account balance, it also led to a virtual disinvestment of the country (Cardoso and Dornbusch, 1991; Institute of International Finance, 1992).

The new government policies forced a precipitous drop in the cost of Brazil's foreign debt. In 1988, the government initiated several new policies to take advantage of the depressed market prices. Brazil commenced repurchasing foreign debt instruments on the open market at discounted prices. It then launched a debt-equity swap program by which it issued shares in some of the larger state companies, such as Telebras and Petrobras. The new initiatives reduced foreign debt by approximately $6 billion, and the total debt principal fell approximately 5%, from $118 billion to around $112 billion; however, they also pushed secondary debt prices up to the point that it was no longer feasible to use the strategy. The process was finally stopped at the start of the 1990s, when the government began negotiating the rescheduling of the foreign debt, thereby pushing secondary market prices even higher.

A comparative analysis of Brazil's foreign debt (see Table 16) shows that, in nominal terms, its foreign obligations were the largest in the region. However, when normalized by GDP, they were not much larger than the other debt levels in the Southern Cone region (see Table 17). In fact, during the year that Brazil was attempting to privatize Telebras (1991), the foreign debt levels were the lowest in the region. However, the servicing of the debt, when normalized by exports (Table 18), was relatively high. Hence, the financing pressures for the government may have provided strong incentives to divest the large state-owned companies.

Table 16
Foreign Debt Levels in the Southern Cone, 1985–1992 (billions U.S. $)

	1985	1986	1987	1988	1989	1990	1991	1992
Brazil	108,040	114,000	123,975	115,458	15,679	21,251	123,287	130,000
Argentina	52,800	54,780	63,050	62,167	63,734	61,187	65,958	70,000
Chile	20,530	20,830	20,660	18,960	17,520	18,576	17,360	19,000
Uruguay	4,900	5,240	5,888	6,331	6,994	7,383	7,167	7,697

Source: International Institute of Finance, 1992–1994.

Table 17
Foreign Debt Levels in the Southern Cone, 1985–1992 (as % of GDP)

	1985	1986	1987	1988	1989	1990	1991	1992
Brazil	48	43	42	35	26	26	30	32
Argentina	60	52	80	71	102	61	45	31
Chile	128	123	109	85	69	66	55	46
Uruguay	103	90	80	83	87	88	73	65

Source: International Institute of Finance, 1992–1994.

Table 18
Foreign Debt Service Levels, 1985–1992
(including amortization as % of total exports)

	1985	1986	1987	1988	1989	1990	1991	1992
Brazil	44	57	48	44	41	43	45	32
Argentina	59	54	73	65	77	64	58	32
Chile	51	47	35	29	27	27	24	22
Uruguay	65	38	39	31	34	35	33	29

Source: International Institute of Finance, 1992–1994.

Multilateral Lending Agencies

The third macroeconomic incentive to privatize came from multilateral lending agencies that pressured Latin American countries to divest state companies. Faced with a slate full of developing countries in poor economic conditions, the IMF and World Bank openly recommended the use of privatization and SOE reform (Armijo, 1994). These organizations established policy-based lending facilities that induced developing countries to pursue structural reforms. For example, the IMF linked its standby arrangements to the macroeconomic performance of each country. Countries were virtually forced into signing letters of intent in which they promised to achieve certain performance goals in growth, fiscal balance, inflation, and trade. Failure to meet the goals resulted in no disbursement of funds. Most of the other multilateral lending agencies also hinged their loans on the successful completion of the IMF goals. By the late 1980s, the major requirement mandated by most of the multilateral agencies was structural adjustment and privatization.

Although multilaterals were one of the few sources of capital available in the region, the Brazilian government was not very interested in being bound to politically unfeasible programs. Ever since 1982, when it was forced to sign a letter of intent with the IMF, Brazil has shied away from multilateral loans. The 1982 loan provided $5.4 billion in new money and allowed the rollover of $5 billion in principal payments, but the country was not able to meet the austere fiscal deficit and inflation targets. Although the multilaterals attempted to keep the lines of communication open with the Brazilian government, there was little hope for adjustment. Interestingly, in 1989, the IMF announced that it would not provide Brazil with additional funds. IMF Managing Director

Michel Camdessus indicated that new lending instruments would not be provided until the country implemented a reasonable economic program (United
Press International, 1989). Therefore, multilateral lending agencies had little
impact on actual Brazilian policies. As Table 19 illustrates, Brazil's net foreign borrowings were negative for the late 1980s, meaning that it was forced to
repay existing loans.

Table 19
Multilateral Net External Borrowing, 1986–1992 (millions U.S.$)

	1986	1987	1988	1989	1990	1991	1992
Argentina							
IMF	159	615	22	-485	-252	-589	-75
World Bank	274	662	329	91	187	69	-145
Other Multilateral	120	131	97	293	320	83	-40
Brazil							
IMF	-616	-1133	-438	-811	-764	-566	-360
World Bank	1004	39	30	-61	-474	-203	-682
Other Multilateral	64	26	112	33	79	-125	59
Chile							
IMF	115	-72	-67	-21	-208	-196	-203
World Bank	334	278	201	100	132	44	66
Other Multilateral	92	188	195	216	337	133	255
Uruguay							
IMF	4	-58	-63	-98	-112	-41	0
World Bank	21	39	24	36	8	38	129
Other Multilateral	18	41	30	35	21	112	3

Sources: World Bank, 1992; International Institute of Finance, 1992–1994.

POLITICAL FACTORS

The sections on the microeconomic and macroeconomic factors surrounding the attempt to privatize Telebras revealed that the government was
unsuccessful in selling the telephone company in 1991. The data and evidence
suggested that the company management assembled an impressive telecommunications conglomerate but operated the firm in an inefficient manner.
Furthermore, the Brazilian economy was plagued by severe fiscal deficits,
macroeconomic distortions, and a large foreign debt; thus it could have bene-
fited from the sale of Telebras. Despite the strong economic pressures to privatize the firm, the government could not amass the political power to sell the

company. Hence, this section analyzes the political factors surrounding the privatization attempt of the telephone company in order to probe for a more complete understanding of the outcome. It specifically examines the roles of the national executive, interest groups, and institutional constraints in shaping the process.

The National Executive

As Brazil entered the 1990s, it was still recovering from a two-decade-long period of authoritarian rule. The military coup of April 1965 toppled the democratically elected government but allowed some of the democratic institutions to continue functioning in a much weaker state. Later in 1965, the military government dissolved all existing political parties and replaced them with two official parties: the government party, the National Renewal Alliance (Aliança Renovadora Nacional—Arena), and a single opposition party, (Movimento Democratico Brasileiro—MDB), which latter evolved into the mainstream Partido Movimento Democratico Brasileiro (PMDB) party. However, groups led by the Catholic Church, lawyers, and journalists increased their opposition to the military throughout the 1960s and 1970s. Eventually a division emerged within the military between hard-liners and those wishing to resurrect civil society (O'Donnell and Schmitter, 1986). By 1974, the military leadership was finally forced to open up the political system, and on November 22, 1979, the two military-approved parties were dissolved and a more liberal party system was inaugurated (Hagopian, 1990). The authoritarian regime gradually began to allow more diverse political groups to emerge and greater levels of political participation; however, the military exercised precise control over the redemocratization process (Stepan, 1986).

Finally, on May 9, 1985, the military regime came to an end when it authorized the Congress to enact a bill restoring all political parties and direct presidential elections. The first president, however, was to be elected indirectly. Unfortunately, Brazil's democratic institutions were left in a disorganized and weakened state. For the most part, the political party system and the Congress were only hollow institutions with few links to traditional social bases. Hagopian (1990) argues that the Brazilian legislature was weakened in relation to the executive and that parties never adequately framed and represented the interest groups. Furthermore, subsequent events undermined the office of the presidency.

Tancredo Neves, a candidate from the left-of-center PMDB party, was the victor in the 1985 indirect presidential election. On the eve of his inauguration, he fell ill and died soon afterward. He was replaced by José Sarney, his vice presidential candidate and a longtime supporter of the military regime. Sarney, however, lacked broad political support. He was from the pro-military PDS party and lacked a strong personality. While Neves had promised to privatize the large state-owned companies and reform the public sector, his successor lacked the initiative to make much progress in either area.

In February 1986, Sarney launched the Cruzado Plan, a heterodox stabilization plan that momentarily eradicated Brazil's inflation and boosted his popularity; it soon failed due to an uncontrolled expansion of demand resulting from wage, monetary, and fiscal policies (Cardoso and Helwege, 1992). In November 1986, the government followed up with the Cruzado II Plan. This plan also failed, as did two other stabilization programs, thus plunging the country into virtual economic chaos (Lal and Maxfield, 1993). The ill-fated programs not only weakened the economy but also undermined the general perception of the presidency and its ability to implement policies and control the economy. President Sarney's popularity plummeted in the polls, and he served out the remaining four years of his term isolated in the official residence, Planoalto.

In 1989, Brazil prepared for a new round of elections, and there was widespread hope that a new leader would emerge. This was the first open presidential election since 1960. On October 3, 1989, over two dozen candidates, from almost as many political parties, presented themselves for the presidency. With no strong parties to mobilize the electorate, it was no surprise that no one candidate was able to secure a majority in the first round. Therefore, the election entered a second round of voting that pitted the two top contenders, Luis Inacio Lula da Silva and Fernando Collor de Mello.

Lula was an union leader from São Paulo who had risen through the ranks and gained national recognition by confronting the military (Alves, 1989). In 1979, he founded the PT and subsequently built it into one of the most viable Brazilian political organizations during the 1980s (Koehnlein, 1994). The party had a clear ideology based on left-of-center principles and a strong grassroots support structure that could be quickly mobilized for electoral campaigns. Indeed, the PT won a number of victories in congressional, mayoral, and gubernatorial races, including control of Brazil's principal industrial city, São Paulo. Hence, the party was ready to seek national leadership.

The other top contender in the 1989 election was Collor, a rich, photogenic, but unknown senator from the impoverished state of Alagoas. Collor was a sophisticated campaigner and ran a high-tech campaign that deftly used opinion polls and expensive television spots; however, he had no political base. In fact, his political party, the National Reconstruction Party (Partido da Reconstrução Nacional—PRN) was a campaign vehicle created to propel him to the presidency. His only apparent source of political support was the media giants, such as the O Globo network. There were other supporters, but many decided to remain in the background. Collor's close associate and campaign manager, Paulo Cesar Farias, built up a network of political supporters by openly selling promises of political favors and patronage (Power, 1994).

The Collor team ran an aggressive campaign that was based on personal appeal and emotions. Collor portrayed himself as an outsider crusading for change; however, he also pandered to the public's fears about economic uncertainty, government mismanagement, racial tension, and class warfare. Much of his rhetoric was focused on the so-called maharajas, the extremely rich and omnipotent managers of the huge state companies. He promised to implement public-sector reforms, eliminate corruption, and increase social spending. On the eve of the election he began to use smear tactics, accusing Lula of infidelity and of having fathered an illegitimate daughter. Faced with the choice of either a messianic senator or an avowed socialist, at the last minute the PMDB decided to throw its full support behind Collor, thus pushing him over the top (Resende-Santos, 1994). On November 15, 1989, Collor collected 35 million votes (53%), defeating Lula and the PT by some 4 million votes (Packenham, 1994). Unwilling to throw the country into political chaos by disputing the election, Lula accepted the results; however, the PT became resolute in its opposition to the new government.

The newly elected Collor administration announced that it was clearly committed to a wholesale reform of the Brazilian economy. The designated Economy Minister, Zelia Cardoso, vowed that she would privatize the electricity, telecommunications, and transportation firms within a year. Indeed, the administration's goal was to raise $18 billion through the sale of 27 companies. This ambitious program required considerable political support, but Collor had won the campaign only through the use of the media. He had failed to gain strategic support from traditional political power bases, such as organized groups or political parties. Furthermore, Collor had no clear mandate to privatize the economy. While his presidential campaign had popularized a negative view of the state and made liberalism more acceptable, he had not campaigned on a specific program of divestiture (Schneider, 1992).

Surveys conducted during the campaign appeared to show that there was strong support for privatization. In early 1990, 43% of those polled in one survey supported privatization. In another poll, 49% favored expanding the private sector, as opposed to 33% who favored state-enterprise growth. It is important to note, however, that nearly two-thirds of the respondents in the survey did not have a clear definition of privatization (Schneider, 1992). It was a term that many individuals had heard in the debates, and it was a policy that was associated with individual candidates, but few understood that it meant the divestiture of state companies. In fact, there was very little support among national elites for the sale of state assets. In 1990, a survey by the Instituto de Estudos Sociais, Economicos, e Politicos de São Paulo (IDESP) of 450 individuals from business, media, academic, political, business, labor, and military groups showed that support for privatization was very weak (Schneider, 1992). Indeed, previous attempts by the Sarney administration to privatize large state owned enterprises had almost been disastrous (Mendes, 1987).

On arrival in Brasilia, the federal capital, on March 15, 1990, the new administration received a lukewarm reception from the traditional parties and political organizations. Collor formed a multiparty ruling coalition in the legislature that included the PMDB—the largest party in the Congress, with approximately 21% of the seats in the lower house—but his PRN party controlled only 8% of the seats (see Table 20). Despite the absence of strong party support, Collor immediately commenced an aggressive and controversial program of policy reforms. Within hours of his inauguration, he signed 22 decrees and launched the so-called Collor Plan. The new stabilization plan froze bank accounts in excess of $650 and eliminated 7,000 federal jobs (5% of the public sector). In his first week in office, he abolished 11 state firms and 13 government agencies (Schneider, 1992).

Table 20
Composition of Lower House During Telebras Privatization Attempt

Party	Number of Seats	Percentage
PMDB	109	21.4
PFL	92	18.0
PDT	46	9.1
PRN	41	8.0
PDS	40	7.9
PSDB	37	7.3
PT	33	6.5
PSP	12	2.3
Others	93	19.5
Total	503	100.0

Source: Banks, 1993.

Collor realized that without the necessary congressional support to pass these programs, he would have to move fast. Therefore, he did not try to use the standard methodology of introducing bills to pass new laws, instead relying on the use of presidential decrees (Power, 1994). This move further eroded his political support in the Congress, however, and within two weeks of his inauguration, the Congress—disregarding the honeymoon period—began rebelling against the steady stream of decrees. Rather than risk delays from prolonged negotiations with the Congress and thus lose control of the economic reforms, Collor ordered his staff to increase the pace of issuing decrees and to even resubmit decrees that had been rejected by the Congress, a serious violation of the Constitution. The tactic further antagonized the Congress, and brought the judiciary into the conflict because of his flagrant disregard for constitutional law. The result was political gridlock and a dramatic slowdown in the pace of economic reforms.

Despite his promise to privatize one company per week, Collor did not sell a single state company until 18 months into his term (Abreu and Werneck, 1993). The government was finally able to sell 16 major companies, mostly in the steel and petrochemical industries, for approximately $3.3 billion, but it had become an embattled administration surrounded by hostile opponents (Baer and Villela, 1992). Economy Minister Cardoso attempted to privatize Telebras through the use of a decree signed by President Sarney. It established the conditions for private companies to exploit "restricted" public services in mobile telephony and satellite channels. The administration wanted to use the decree as a loophole to increase competition in the telecommunications sector and allow for greater private sector participation in the ownership of state companies (*Latin America Weekly Report*, 1990). The initiative was immediately challenged by the union of Telebras workers, who brought the matter before Congress and the Supreme Court. The administration, however, never had an opportunity to respond to the challenge because the president was impeached on September 29, 1992. Therefore, the initiative did not fail because of overwhelming opposition to the sale of the telephone company; it stagnated due to the overwhelming antagonism of the Congress toward the administration.

Interest Groups

Although, the PT led much of the opposition against the Collor administration, the power of the Congress to oppose the president was poor and largely untested. The Congress, as an independent political institution, had suffered greatly under the military government. Hagopian (1990) has argued that the military ensured that the new political system left the country with weak democratic institutions while reserving substantial formal and informal powers to itself. Military officers demanded consultation on policy issues, including economic ones. For example, their opposition to the sale of the strategic state-owned companies has been one of the major obstacles to the program. Furthermore, the party system in Brazil has traditionally been weak and fragmented (Stepan, 1978). Ever since the period of the Estado Nôvo (1937–1945), the government had centralized economic and political control in the hands of the state bureaucracy (Payne, 1994) .

Although the legislature was not suspended during the military regime, it was emasculated by the Second Institutional Act (AI-2), issued in October 1965 (Power, 1994). It allowed military leaders to recess all legislative bodies at will and legislate in their absence. This basically lowered a permanent guillotine over the heads of the Congress and reduced it to a virtual rubber stamp. Under the leadership of General Humberto de Alencar Castello Branco, the military government used decrees to legislate issues concerning most matters of national security, public finance, and administration (Payne, 1994). Hence, during the next 20 years, the legislature lost all of its deliberative powers, abilities, and practices. The return to democratic rule allowed the Congress to resume some of its traditional powers and characteristics, but the proliferation of parties in the Senate and the lower house disseminated and diffused political power across a wide spectrum (see Table 21). Disappointed with the institution, absenteeism among members grew, as did the level of corruption (Teixeira, 1989; Manzetti, 1994).

Table 21
Composition of Senate During Telebras Privatization Attempt

Party	Number of Seats	Percentage
PMDB	26	32.4
PFL	14	17.2
PDS	10	12.3
PTB	6	7.4
PDT	5	6.1
PSDB	4	4.9
PRN	4	4.9
Others	12	14.8
Total	81	100.0

At the time of the privatization attempt, the overall congressional support for privatization policies was lukewarm at best. Some members of Congress, such as Renato Johnson, supported the privatization of the telephone company. Johnson indicated that privatization was necessary to provide the level of investment that the company needed for expansion (*Latin Finance*, 1992). Mainwaring (1994) has argued that the minority situations of Brazilian presidents have often led to difficulties and impasses between the executive and the legislature. The legislature and executive have often reached agreement on some major issues, but also have been deadlocked over some of the more controversial issues.

The pockets of privatization support in the general business community, however, were few. Bartell (1993) argues that the lack of enthusiasm for privatization in the business community was largely due to the long corporatist tradition in Brazil and the clientelistic economic relations among government, labor, and business.[5] Payne's (1994) analysis of Brazilian industrialists found them somewhat well organized but divided on many issues. However, one issue on which they were united was privatization. The business sector in Brazil viewed state-intervention in the production side of the market as a vital condition for economic expansion. By allowing the government to set up large national companies, they could then assemble a vast network of industrial activities to provide equipment and support.

The suppliers of telecommunications equipment were no different. They derived significant benefits from the provision of supplies and services to the state telephone company. Wajnberg (1992) reports that in 1991, the sector consisted of 120 firms employing 35,200 individuals and generating $1.37 billion in revenues. Furthermore, there was an outright fear among many business elites that privatization would result in the divestiture of strategic state companies to foreigners. One of the only public backers of the Telebras sale was Roberto Marinho, the owner of the O Globo television network, a strong backer of Collor, and a partner in Viacom (a satellite communication company) and NEC-Brazil (mobile telephony), who sought to buy the company in conjunction with major U.S. telephone companies.

Although the backers of the privatization program were disorganized, the opposition group was not much better. The opposition to the privatization of Telebras was led by the PT. Allied with the PT were the powerful unions of state-managed companies and myriad grassroots movements formed during the military dictatorship. Since the party was comprised of labor unions, socialist groups, and grassroots associations, it was often divided on specific policy issues. Furthermore, the labor union structure in Brazil has traditionally been weak. Mericle (1977) showed that there was no peak labor association in Brazil like those in Chile and Argentina. Last, other opponents of the privatization of Telebras included most Telebras managers.

Institutional Constraints

In the absence of a strong executive, Congress, or powerful interest groups to lead or oppose the privatization process, then the institutional rules became very important in shaping the Telebras outcome. Two institutions were especially important in the privatization attempt of the company: the 1988 Constitution and the National Bank for Economic and Social Development (Banco Nacional de Desenvolvimento Economico e Social [BNDES]). However, the former was probably more important than the latter.

One of the demands presented to the military regime during the early 1980s was the convening of a national assembly to rewrite the Brazilian Constitution so that it would provide the basis for the new democratic regime.[6] A year after the election of the first civilian president, a new Congress was elected in 1986; it also sat as the National Constituent Assembly (Power, 1994). The members of the convention designed a plan that would prevent a repeat of the authoritarian regime, a plan that was a reaction to several of the more controversial policies of the day. One such policy was the privatization of the large state-owned enterprises. Many members of the assembly realized that a strong president would have no problem privatizing strategic firms such as Petrobras and Telebras. In order to prevent or delay such an event, an amendment was entered into Title VII of the Constitution that prevented the sale of these companies (Souto, 1990). Hence, it would take a constitutional amendment to allow the sale of Telebras. The amendment process, however, provided a strong challenge to any future administration seeking to sell these companies. Article 60 of the Constitution stipulated that any amendment would require a quorum of three-fifths of both congressional chambers, the House of Deputies and Senate, for two sessions, to deliberate the issue, and the approval of three-fifths of the members from both houses to pass the amendment.

The other institution that could have shaped the Telebras outcome was BNDES. It was one of the strongest backers of privatization policies in the country (Schneider, 1989). The Brazilian development bank had a large portfolio of previously private firms that had defaulted on their debts. BNDES personnel were some of strongest proponents of economic structural reforms and divestiture of state companies. Hence, the agency's technocrats were placed in charge of the privatization program. They drafted schedules, performed company audits, and managed the selling process (BNDES, 1991). However, they were legally prohibited from becoming involved with the privatization of the strategic state companies. Strategic companies were independent organizations that reported directly to the national executive through their respective ministries (Mendes, 1987). State companies grew very independent under the military regime, and the military leaders appointed the company executives so as to insulate them from political meddling by federal and state governments (Gil-Garcia, 1993; Teixeira, 1989). Indeed, Lal and Maxfield (1993) observed that these strategic state companies enjoyed a political and institutional independence that afforded them financial autonomy. Therefore, in the face of political weakness by both the proponents and the opponents of the Telebras privatization, it was the rules of Brazilian institutions that shaped the process and outcome.

CONCLUSION

The analysis of the microeconomic, macroeconomic, and political factors of the Brazilian case yields interesting results. From a microeconomic perspective, Telebras was clearly an impressive SOE. It was very large and had developed an impressive domestic telecommunications sector. The company, however, was inefficient. While the company's top management had the best intentions to implement good policies, there was too much political manipulation at the local level by powerful interest groups. The latter included industrial groups and labor organizations. These same groups created a powerful opposition force to the privatization initiative. Nevertheless, the microeconomic conditions should have created a positive environment for privatization because the company could have boosted performance.

The same can be said for the macroeconomic factors. Brazil suffered a severe macroeconomic crisis during most of the 1980s. Government policies resulted in explosively high fiscal deficits, inflation rates, and foreign debt levels. By the end of the decade, they also produced low growth patterns. Furthermore, the country faced intensive pressure from international lending

agencies to privatize. These conditions help explain why Brazil's leadership so
strongly debated the issue of privatization, but cannot explain why the country
did not divest its state companies, especially the large strategic units.

While the economic factors suggest that the privatization of Telebras
should have been probable, the political analysis yields a different result. Indeed, the country suffers from weak political institutions. Brazil's democratic
institutions were weakened by the military governments. Furthermore, the
traditions of the first two presidents endorsed this apparent weakness. The absence of political leadership helped explain why many of the economic stabilization and structural adjustment programs of the 1980s and 1990s stagnated
and eventually failed (Pereira, 1994). The privatization program also was constrained by many of the country's institutional rules, such as the constitutional
prohibition of the sale of strategic state companies. Therefore, despite the presence of pro-privatization economic conditions, Brazil's weak political condition
prevented the sale of the state-owned telephone company. Telebras would indeed have been a good privatization candidate, but the national leadership
could not carry out the process.

NOTES

1. Lerner (1991) argues that the privatization of the telecommunications sector
helps reduce many of the structural impediments, thus improving competition and
leading to increased productivity.

2. The telecommunications industry became a highly politicized issue in the
1960s. In February 1962, Leonel Brizola, the governor of Rio Grande do Sul, nationalized the ITT-owned telephone company in Pôrto Alegre (Schoenberg, 1985). Although
President Joao Goulart later reimbursed the company for full value, the subject of foreign ownership of the telephone companies was becoming a contentious issue.

3. For a more detailed analysis of state-led development, see the literature on
import-substitution industrialization (ISI).

4. Cardoso and Fishlow (1988) underlined the Brazilian situation by showing
that $35 billion of the debt accumulated between 1978 and 1982 was due to higher oil
prices and reduced commodity prices.

5. Gomes (1994) argues that Companhia Brasileira do Comercio Exterior
(Concex) is one of the strongest business organizations in the country. While the export-oriented sectors of Brazilian industry are very well organized, the peak business
groups in Brazil such as FIESP have declined in prominence since the end of the military rule. Furthermore, they did not demonstrate a strong preference for privatization
policies because many member firms provided equipment and services to the large state
companies.

6. Of course such concessions came at a price. In exchange for the departure
of the military and the drafting of a new constitution, the military extracted promises
that it would never be prosecuted for civil rights violations and that it would always
retain an oversight role (Hagopian, 1990).

3

CHILE

OVERVIEW

Privatization in Chile dates back to the mid-1970s, when military forces under the command of General Augusto Pinochet ousted the civilian government. The coup was a response to the radical transformation of the Chilean economy by the left-of-center Popular Front movement. Salvador Allende, elected president in 1970, implemented new policies to alter the structure of the Chilean economy. Price controls were introduced, firms were nationalized, and protectionist policies were implemented. In 1973, the military put an end to these policies by overthrowing the democratically elected government. The military reversed most of Allende's policies and ended the country's short socialist experiment. The new government immediately initiated a round of privatizations to trim the fiscal deficit and eliminate the macroeconomic disequilibrium that had been introduced by the prior administration. It also initiated a process of privatization. The government divested most of the smaller companies and banks that had been expropriated by the state between 1970 and 1973, except for the large enterprises such as airlines, mining operations, and public utilities which were privatized a decade later (Hachette and Lüders, 1988). Of the 500 companies that were under state ownership in the early 1970s, only 19 remained under public control by the end of the decade (Yotopoulos, 1989). However, by the mid-1980s, the Chilean government launched another round of privatizations that included Compañia de Teléfonos de Chile (CTC).

In 1984 the military government, bowing to domestic and international political and economic pressure, launched simultaneous programs of re-democratization and more privatizations. The former gradually expanded political participation to other social groups, but with the intent of maintaining the military in control until the end of the century. The latter was designed to remove the more powerful resources, such as the large SOEs, from the hands of future civilian governments (Stallings and Brock, 1993). This would ensure the preservation of the free-market economic reforms installed after the coup. In August 1987, the Chilean government announced the privatization of CTC, the state-owned telephone company. Six months later, 151 million common "A" shares of CTC stock were sold to the Bond Corporation of Chile, which offered $114.8 million in cash and debt instruments, thereby giving it full ownership and control of the company. The Bond Corporation was the holding company of Australian financier Alan Bond, a media tycoon.

MICROECONOMIC FACTORS

Formation and Early History

CTC was the first provider of telephone services in Chile. The firm was established in Valparaiso in 1880, and by 1881 it had a network of 300 telephones. In 1884, CTC entered into a joint venture with a U.S. partner, the West Coast Telephone Company. Five years later, the Chilean company acquired the West Coast Telephone Company, increasing the firm's total lines to 2,187 (Melo, 1992). By 1927, CTC had grown to 26,205 lines and was sold to the North American firm, International Telephone and Telegraph (ITT). ITT was a large conglomerate that owned telephone operating companies and equipment manufacturing facilities throughout the world.

As in most developing countries, the Chilean network was centered mainly in the major economic urban centers, and long-distance operations were limited. The long-distance network in Chile consisted of a sole connection between Santiago and the port of Valparaíso; but the absence of an expansive long-distance network became painfully apparent during the crisis surrounding a devastating earthquake of 1960. Due to the absence of a telecommunications system, many towns in the southern part of the country were isolated from rescue efforts. Coupled with heightened military tensions with Argentina during the same period, the government finally created a state-owned long-distance company, Entel. The establishment of Entel in 1964 marked a new trend in government intervention in the telecommunications industry. In 1967, the government announced a national telecommunications policy that increased its control of all network operations through the state development agency, Corporacion de Fomento de la Produccion (CORFO). It was authorized to increase its control of CTC by purchasing 49% of the firm's stock (Galal, 1993).

CORFO had been in existence since the early 1940s, when it was created to foster the development of Chilean productive activities through loans and guarantees to the private sector. In 1970, CORFO held an equity stake in 46 companies; this had increased to 500 companies by 1973, when the socialist government began an expanded program of nationalization. CORFO's acquisitions were usually implemented through the capitalization of government taxes, receivership, or seizing control through nationalization.

In 1970, the Allende government decided to wrest managing control of CTC from ITT. On May 26, 1971, the government informed ITT that it would begin steps to nationalize CTC. This led to the now famous plea from the multinational corporation to the U.S. government and the subsequent alleged involvement by the CIA in toppling the Allende administration (Sampson, 1973).[1] On September 29, 1971, the government formally intervened in the company by appointing an overseer. ITT was offered $24 million for its assets, which had recently been valued at $153 million (Schoenberg, 1985). Formal nationalization of the firm, however, never occurred under the Allende government; it came shortly after the coup. Late in 1973, the operating contract for CTC was revoked by the U.S. supported military government, and in 1974 the military-controlled CORFO acquired the remaining shares from ITT for $125.2 million.

Political Control

As in Brazil, political control of the Chilean telephone industry was minimal during its early years; however, it did not increase very much after the government assumed ownership of the company in 1974. Between 1880 and 1974, the telecommunications industry was under private ownership, regulated by a specific operating contract. The original concession for CTC provided the telephone operator with a fifty-year license. The company was allowed to charge telephone rates that provided a maximum rate of return of 10%. Nonetheless, the government retained some political control. It appointed three of the fifteen company directors, and there were limitations on nationality—80% of the company staff had to be Chileans.

The firm continued to operate relatively free of political manipulation even after its acquisition by the military. ITT was paid a generous fee to manage the firm until new Chilean managers could be trained. Although CTC was now owned by the government, the company remained subject to private-sector accounting and reporting rules (Hachette and Lüders, 1988). In the late 1970s, the government began some political manipulation by integrating the tariffs of Entel and CTC. Since both companies were owned by CORFO, the state was able to set up a cross-subsidization scheme similar to that in the United States, whereby long-distance rates subsidized local urban services (Castillo, 1993).

Firm Performance

In the late 1960s, the civilian management of CTC perceived a deterioration of relations with the government. With political rhetoric rising and the government increasing its stake in the company, the management decided to decrease its level of investment. By the start of the 1970s, however, the lack of investment halted the firm's rate of growth and its performance began to deteriorate. The financial crisis that hit Chile in the early 1980s exacerbated the situation by limiting the growth of the network, leading to an explosive rise in the telephone installation backlog.

The Chilean telephone system clearly suffered from a lack of investment and new resources. As shown in Table 7, it ranked fourth in line penetration compared with other companies in the Southern Cone; nonetheless, the firm's management maintained a sound financial performance. CTC averaged the highest revenue per line in the four countries. Therefore, CTC's problem was not mismanagement but lack of investment.

Technology

The relatively small size of Chile's population, economy, and telephone network, denied the economies of scale needed to proceed with the import-substitution experiments that were implemented by some of the larger Latin American countries. Most of Chile's industrialization was devoted to fishing and copper mining—areas where the country had a comparative advantage. Despite the absence of an indigenous telecommunications industry, Chilean planners focused on developing a technologically advanced telephone network. Chile's rugged terrain and great expanses could be overcome only with technological sophistication, thus encouraging investment in microwave technology as a major format for long-distance communications (Castillo, 1993). The establishment of Entel, the state-owned long-distance carrier, led to heavy investment in technology and network expansion. As shown in Table 8, the Chilean network had the highest level of digitalization in the Southern Cone.

Investment and Financing

Because CTC was relatively efficient and well-managed, the small size of the network prevented the company from accessing domestic or international capital markets for investment. Most investment programs relied on self-financing from tariffs and government loans. Despite the limited resources, the company's management was able to implement a consistent investment plan in technology. Nonetheless, as can be seen in Table 9, the overall rate of investment declined in the year prior to privatization. The company's thin resources were unable to keep up with growing demand. Therefore, investment became one of the cornerstones of the privatization program. Bidding companies had to commit to install an additional 1.2 million lines by December 31, 1992 (CTC, 1990).

Labor

During the 1960s and until the military coup of 1973, labor was an important economic and political force in Chile, but the military coup reversed that. The new government demobilized organized labor and commenced repressive actions against union leadership. The result was a de-facto deregulation of the labor market due to the unions' loss of power. By 1980, union membership had dropped by almost half, thus emasculating labor's political power. In 1983, however, the redemocratization of Chile allowed organized labor to reemerge. In 1986, the only organized labor force that survived the military regime was the powerful Copper Confederation, and it led the first protests against the government (Angell, 1991). Although repressive actions still continued against labor, the unions entered into a dialogue with the government about the terms and conditions of privatization. A major concession by the government was setting aside 10% of the privatized companies shares for sale to the workers.

CTC's use of labor was relatively efficient compared with the other cases. In the years prior to the 1987 privatization, it ranked among the most efficient telephone companies in Latin America (see Table 10). Its revenue per employee ranked behind Brazil, but its lines per employee figure was the highest in the region. A massive restructuring by the new private-sector owners of the company allowed its performance to improve even more.

MACROECONOMIC FACTORS

Fiscal Performance and Inflation

The years leading up to the military intervention witnessed the creation of a massive macroeconomic disequilibrium in Chile. The Unidad Popular (UP) government, headed by Salvador Allende, aggressively expanded the state sector. Unfortunately, the expansion exceeded the capacity of the economy and the government. The expansion program was led by CORFO, a national development organization that was designed to provide long-term financing, guarantees, and consulting services to Chilean firms. At the instigation of UP party militants, CORFO developed a policy of nationalization. By 1970, the state agency held an equity stake in forty-six companies, mostly as a result of converting public loans into shares. Between 1970 and 1973, the number of firms under CORFO control climbed to 500. This followed the takeover of 259 companies and the acquisition of another 204, including 19 commercial banks, increasing the government's ownership five fold.

The Allende government attempted to finance the expansion of the public sector by raising new taxes, but it could not get political support from the Congress (Hachette and Lüders, 1992). Hence, it resorted to using Central Bank reserves to finance its economic programs. The burgeoning public-sector deficit was also financed through monetary expansion and foreign loans. Soon the public deficit exploded to 24.7% of GDP and inflation grew to 487% year-on-year (Budnevich, 1993). The administration tried to protect domestic industries and halt the economic crisis by erecting high import barriers, and price and exchange controls. Unfortunately, these measures resulted only in the breakdown of pricing structures and market mechanisms. Thus, there ensued a massive decline in growth, a dramatic reduction in investment, and a liquidation of foreign reserves as capital fled the country.

By 1973, the economic problems had come to a head. The efficient administration of SOEs collapsed, and much of the productive system fell into disorder. Although Chilean SOEs were once very well managed, most of the original managers had been ousted or had fled the country. Many firms stopped preparing annual reports, and payrolls became highly politicized. By the end of the Allende administration, approximately 85% of the financial and mining sectors, 40% of the industrial sector, and 55% of the agricultural sector were in the hands of the government (Glade, 1989).

In 1973, the new military administration attempted to reverse the situation by enforcing a series of proactive measures to reduce the level of government spending and stabilize the economy. Under the leadership of the finance minister, and a University of Chicago economist, named Sergio de Castro, the new government removed price controls and demobilized labor unions.[2] Although the administration sought to stabilize the economy, it maintained reasonable anti-inflation goals while focusing on the development of the external sector and market-oriented strategies (Ritter, 1990). The new measures, however, produced a severe recession in 1975, and the economy contracted by 12.9%. Fortunately, the period of adjustment was over within a year, and the economy quickly rebounded. Between 1976 and 1981, the Chilean economy grew 7.1%.

The new economic regime forced state-owned enterprises to rationalize their business practices. The government no longer assumed company liabilities and cost overruns. Hence, each SOE was required to operate as if it were a private firm. This required SOEs to balance their books and practice self-financing. Between 1973 and 1978, the government took the new measures one step further by initiating a profound privatization program that transferred 500 firms to the private sector. Not only did this eliminate over one-third of the fiscal deficit, it also added over $1 billion to the state coffers (Hachette and Lüders, 1992).

While the government thoroughly liberalized the economy, it failed to introduce important regulations and safeguards to monitor the newly expanded private sector. One area that was radically deregulated, but also grossly under-monitored, was banking (Brock, 1992). With domestic interest rates soaring due to tight monetarist policies, and the currency showing increasing signs of overvaluation, Chilean banks obtained cheap capital by borrowing abroad.[3] Hence, they were able to finance a wave of highly leveraged acquisitions by the banks. But the period of high international liquidity and low international interest rates ended with the Mexican debt crisis, and soon many Chilean financial institutions were in trouble.

In 1982, the banking sector plunged the country into another economic crisis as loan portfolios fell apart. The world recession of 1982 exacerbated the situation by depressing commodity prices, particularly of copper, and pushing more Chilean firms into financial ruin. Many entrepreneur groups that had bought privatized assets during the 1970s at very cheap prices fell into bankruptcy. The newly privatized firms were unable to service their dollar-based obligations as interest rates climbed. They also lacked the expertise and capital to withstand the economic downturn. Faced with poorly performing loans at home, Chile could not turn to the international market for more capital because of the growing international debt crisis. Hence, the country fell into a recession worse than the 1973 economic crisis; by the end of 1982, the economy had contracted by 14.3% (Pietrobelli, 1994). On January 13, 1983, eight private banks representing 60% of the financial system collapsed and were intervened. The government was also forced to renationalize many of the companies that had recently been privatized (Yotopoulos, 1989).

Chile finally emerged from the economic crisis in 1984–1985. The military government recommenced the process of privatization and divested its portfolio of recently acquired companies (Castillo, 1993). The economy, however, continued to suffer from high levels of unemployment and relatively low levels of investment. Most of these problems were attributed to the macro-economic distortions created by the large SOEs; therefore, the government decided to commence another round of privatizations by selling twenty-nine of the larger strategic firms (Hachette and Lüders, 1992). The new program sought to improve the economic structure by further opening the economy and spurring higher levels of investment.

The privatization initiative was also designed to help reduce the fiscal deficit. However, the fiscal deficit in Chile was different from the one in the Brazil. In Brazil, the fiscal deficit was driven by losses generated by SOEs; however, most Chilean SOEs produced surpluses. Indeed, during the years leading up to the privatization of CTC, the telephone company posted profits each year except 1982 and 1985.[4] Nonetheless, the Chilean public sector was bloated and inefficient. By selling the large SOEs to foreign investors, the government hoped to increase the level of foreign investment, improve overall efficiency and productivity, and increase the level of economic activity—thereby raising government revenues (Marcel, 1989). Hence, fiscal pressures played an important part in the government's decision to privatize the telephone company.[5] As shown in Tables 13 and 14, Chile indeed suffered from moderate fiscal deficits and inflation rates; however, it did not have the low levels of growth seen in the other nations.

Foreign Debt

During the late 1970s, the Chilean government made steady progress in reducing the foreign debt obligations that had accumulated under earlier governments, but the banking and economic crises of the early 1980s erased all of the gains. When the government took control of bankrupt firms during the 1982 crisis, it had to assume responsibility for most foreign credits. Hence, between 1980 and 1983, Chile's foreign debt exploded 50%, from $12 billion to $18 billion (World Bank, 1992).[6] Given its foreign debt burden of 121% of GDP in 1983, Chile could no longer afford to assume any more obligations to expand and modernize state-owned companies. With a relatively low domestic savings rate of 8%, the country remained highly dependent on foreign financing (Larrain, 1992). Hence, the country was forced to stop expanding its industrial base, modernizing its infrastructure, and expanding the economy. Instead, it was forced to grow at a more optimal and slower rate (Ffrench-Davis, 1989). Hence, Chile experienced another period of structural adjustment and privatization. Marcel (1989) argued that indeed the third round of privatizations was driven by the need to access new sources of capital and to create new mechanisms for the conversion of external debt. Therefore, it is clear that Chilean privatization of the telephone company was strongly affected by the country's high level of foreign debt (see Tables 16–18).[7]

In order to maximize the amount of debt that would be used for the privatization program, the government developed a series of debt-equity swap programs. Chapters XVIII and XIX of the Compendium of Rules on Foreign Exchange set the rules for debt-equity conversions. The program had two intentions. The first was to increase foreign investment in Chile, and the second was to increase the repatriation of flight capital that had left during the banking crisis. Chapter XIX applied only to foreign investors or Chileans living abroad. Such investors were allowed to acquire Chilean debt (which was trading at 60% of face value) and then exchange it for equity in state firms that were being privatized. While they could redeem for it 85% of face value, the investment had to remain in the country for ten years, and dividends could not leave the country until the fifth year. Furthermore, all transactions had to be approved by the Central Bank. Chapter XVIII, also known as Annex 4, also was used to capitalize the privatized firms, but it applied only to Chileans living in Chile. Thus, the privatization program allowed Chile to drastically reduce its debt obligation in nominal and real terms.

Multilateral Lending Agencies

The free-market tendencies of the Chilean government put the country in good stead with the multilateral lending agencies, despite accusations of civil rights violations. In fact, most Chilean economic policies were conducted in conjunction with the IMF and the World Bank. As Table 19 indicates, Chile was one of the most consistent recipients of multilateral funds in the region. It received several structural adjustment loans (SALS) from the World Bank, despite increasing political pressure from the United States. Although many members of the U.S. Congress urged the Reagan and Bush administrations to vote against any more World Bank loans, the U.S. government refused to derail one of the few sound economies in the region. With the United States controlling 20% of the voting capital in the World Bank, it had the power to refuse any more lending and destroy the program. However, the most severe action by the U.S. government was abstention, which allowed the approval of the loans.

The IMF also provided loans for the expansion of exports, reduction of the fiscal deficit, and the expansion of the privatization program (EIU, 1987). Since the Chilean economic policies were in line with IMF guidelines, the government was virtually always in compliance, making it easier for other multilaterals to provide loans and credits. Hence, Chile worked closely with the multilateral agencies to promote the privatization initiative.

POLITICAL FACTORS

The National Executive

Since the sale of CTC occurred almost thirteen years after the military takeover of Chile, it is necessary to understand the events that occurred between 1970 and 1973 in order to grasp the political forces that shaped the privatization process. The breakdown of the civilian political institutions during that time period transcends a struggle between the Chilean political left and right. Instead, it was rooted in an inherent flaw that existed within the country's political structure. Unlike Brazil, which centralized power within the national executive and the bureaucracy, the Chilean political system developed a long tradition of relative equilibrium between the presidency and the legislature (Scully, 1992). The system worked well most of the time; however, it broke down when the two institutions came to an impasse. The absence of a third and viable political institution to mediate between the executive branch and the Congress led to the political breakdown of the early 1970s. Although the courts attempted to serve as mediator, they had neither the resources nor the will to broker the crisis, and the military eventually was forced to intervene in order to prevent a full-scale civil war (Valenzuela, 1978). Therefore, it is important to take a deeper look at the political events surrounding this breakdown and the impact it would have on Chile's future political economy.

In 1970, Salvador Allende Gossens was elected president with 36.6% of the vote. Jorge Alessandri, a free-market advocate from the National Party, received 35.2% of the vote, and the centrist Christian Democrat candidate, Radomiro Tomic, came in third with 28.1% of the vote. Since no single candidate received the 50% +1 majority needed to win the election, the Chilean Constitution mandated that the Congress decide between the two top candidates.

The Congress, however, was controlled by the Christian Democrats, who held two-thirds of the seats. But although Allende was from the Unidad Popular party, a coalition of socialist and Marxist groups, the Christian Democrats allowed him to assume the presidency. In return, they received a set of guarantees and concessions that Allende would not change the country's fundamental political institutions. Nonetheless, the more Marxist elements of Unidad Popular disregarded the agreement and immediately began implementing aggressive changes in the country's social, economic, and political structures; and factories, businesses, and farms were appropriated by groups of workers. In 1972, the national courts attempted in vain to reverse many of these illegal seizures by interpreting existing laws and defining property rights. Faced with the strong possibility of a civil war, largely fueled by threats from Marxist elements to arm peasants and workers, the military decided to intervene, and assumed control on September 11, 1973.

It is important to note that once in power, the new military government did not side with any of the competing factions. It immediately dismantled Chile's democratic institutions and vested all political power under a single authoritarian commander, General Augusto Pinochet (Arriagada, 1988). It dismissed the Congress, outlawed political parties, and stripped labor unions of their bargaining and organizational rights. Many civil rights were restricted, including freedom of speech, press, and assembly (Stallings and Brock, 1993). Furthermore, the military jailed and exiled thousands of people. It also prosecuted dissidents, killing several thousand in the process. The military's actions were so extreme that it became alienated from the business community. The military government then began a process of reversing many of the programs implemented by Unidad Popular (Larrain, 1992). Instead of returning economic control to the traditional business forces that had opposed President Allende, the new government came to rely on a cadre of U.S.-trained economists from the Catholic University of Santiago, known as the Chicago Boys.[8]

Giraldo (1994) has argued that the Chicago Boys were determined to reverse many of the redistribution policies that had been implemented since the mid-1930s. They shared with the military a contempt for political parties, politicians, and interest groups. They also shared disdain for the narrow economic interest groups that had precipitated the political and economic crises. Indeed, both groups held in common a perception that interest groups in general prevented the implementation of policies that would benefit the country as a whole. Therefore, the only way to implement the changes needed to *rescue* Chile was through a "benign dictatorship" that would solve the collective action problem. Indeed, Silva (1992) argued that the Chicago Boys and the military were convinced that the only way to transform Chile's economic model was through a complete centralization of power. Therefore, Chile's new rulers were faced with a complex proposition that would take a long time to implement.

In 1976, the military rulers appointed a Council of State to reshape Chile's political institutions, including the drafting of a new constitution. In 1980, a new constitution was voted into place. At the same time, General Pinochet was given an eight-year term that would expire in 1989. With the clock counting down to a return to a democratic environment, the country's rulers decided that they had to move fast to lock in the economic policies imposed since the coup. The centerpiece of this initiative would be the privatization of the remaining state-owned companies. Although there were some important macroeconomic considerations driving the privatization program, the political factors were probably more important.[9] Unwilling to turn over a vast public sector to a future government of unknown political persuasion, the government decided to divest it. To further ensure that these assets remained within the private sector, the government designed a privatization program to give foreign bidders a comparative advantage.[10]

As part of the foreign-debt restructuring program, the Chilean government decided to allow foreigners to purchase shares in Chilean privatization programs through debt-equity swaps. In 1985, the Central Bank introduced several mechanisms to convert foreign debt into equity. One such mechanism, known as Chapter XIX, allowed creditors to convert Chilean foreign debt into equity shares in privatized firms. Another mechanism, called Chapter XVIII, allowed private agents to purchase Chilean debt on the secondary market and use it to pay for equity stakes in privatized companies (Larrain, 1992). Since most Latin American debt was trading on the international markets at a deep discount, foreigners were able to buy privatized Chilean assets at very low prices. The program allowed Chile to retire about $4 billion (almost 25%) of its total debt obligations, and it also provided a lucrative incentive for foreigners to establish large stakes in Chilean firms.[11] In order to lock in the investments for a long period of time, Chilean foreign investment Rule DL600 forced investors to maintain their holdings for a minimum of three years (Sáez, 1992).

The privatization of CTC was a clear example of the advantage that was given to foreign owners. In 1986, CORFO announced that it would sell 51% of the telephone company. The next year, the government sold 6.4% of the shares, to workers and 7.6% to Chilean pension funds. In 1988, CORFO

invited domestic and foreign investors to bid for at least 30% of the shares with
two conditions: the bidders had to commit themselves to subscribe for new
shares so that their final stake would reach at least 45%, that the winner had to
buy over ten million B shares of CTC.[12] In two weeks, Alan Bond, an Austra-
lian financier and speculator, offered $114.8 million for 50.1% of the shares
(see Table 22). Surprisingly, Bond had no experience in the telecommunications industry. The remaining shares were then sold on the international capital markets in the form of American Depository Receipts (ADRs) and Global
Depository Receipts (GDRs). Some of the remaining shares were later sold to
Chileans through the popular privatization program, whereby the government
subsidized the sale of small quantities of company shares to individual investors. Overall, the privatization program prevented the centralization of power
in any single domestic group(s) and thus reduced the chances of creating powerful interest groups.[13]

Table 22
CTC Ownership Structure, 1987–1990

	1987	1988	1989	1990
CORFO	75.0	14.2	2.9	0.1
Private/Domestic				
Pension Funds	7.6	7.7	11.6	11.6
CTC Employees	6.4	4.3	3.2	3.2
Other	10.2	23.5	31.9	25.8
Total	24.2	35.5	46.7	40.6
Foreign				
Bond Corp.	0.0	50.1	49.2	0.0
Telefónica	0.0	0.0	0.0	43.4
ADRs	0.0	0.0	0.0	14.9
Other	0.8	0.2	1.2	1.0
Total	0.8	50.3	50.4	59.4

Source: CTC, 1990.

Interest Groups

During the postwar period, Chile developed a complex political system
of interest group aggregation and representation (Frieden, 1991). Political parties were well defined, and business and labor unions were very well organized.
The associations reached a new height of organization and power in the last
years of the Chilean democracy. It was a time when both business and labor
were able to mobilize themselves and from a unified front. The subsequent
authoritarian government, however, either disbanded or neutralized the groups.
As has been argued in the previous section, both the economic technocrats and
the military leaders disliked the concept of organized interest groups.

The business sector, for example, formed a peak organization called the National Front of the Private Sector (FRENAP) to protest the actions of Unidad Popular during the Allende government (Stallings and Brock, 1993). The business association supported the new military regime during the days leading up to and following the coup, but reduced its support when it became evident that the new economic technocrats would not give preferential treatment to traditional businesses. It muted its opposition to the new military government, however, fearing a return to a leftist government. Subsequent business groups became more interested in shaping government policies on investment rules and exchange regimes, and did not have much say in the privatization policies (Silva, 1992). Hence, the business sector was largely neutralized in regard to the sale of CTC.

The government also replaced most of the prior management in the large public-sector companies with generals, colonels, and economic technocrats (Galal, 1993; Giraldo, 1994). The new management cooperated closely with all of the authoritarian regime policies. Therefore, there was no opposition from the business side or from state-company managers to the privatization of CTC. Furthermore, the absence of a domestic telecommunications equipment industry reduced many of the pressures from the business sector.

The military government also took aim at the unions. Starting in 1973, the new government suppressed union activity through legislation, repression, and often outright brutality. By the early 1980s, the union membership had dropped to one-third of its levels in the early 1970s. Many union leaders were fired, exiled, jailed, or killed. Nonetheless, the labor movement did not entirely disappear. The Chilean Copper Confederation was the strongest union syndicate prior to the coup and remained strong during the ensuing period. In May 1983, copper workers launched the first series of protests against the military regime since the coup. Slowly, they were able to recover much of the power that they had lost during the past decade, and by 1988 they helped create a nation wide labor federation, Central Unitaria de Trabajadores (CUT).[14]

Given the lack of ability to transmit demands to the government, it is no surprise that the government was able to implement the privatization program with no opposition (Ruiz-Tagle, 1989). The rebirth of the labor movement may have forced the government to appease workers through the popular privatization program, but this was also in line with its general policy of atomizing economic and political power. Indeed, this approach was successfully used in the United Kingdom to diffuse company ownership by disseminating shares.[15] Not only did the Chilean popular privatization program allow small investors to purchase small packages of stock, but privatized companies were allowed to set up employee stock ownership plans. Many privately managed pension funds became important purchasers of corporate securities in the newly privatized concerns. Therefore, government strategies effectively neutralized the power of interest groups in Chile, vastly curtailing their ability to organize and negotiate with the government.

Institutional Constraints

The military government dismantled most democratic institutions during the 1970s and early 1980s. It designed new institutions that concentrated power in the chief executive and reduced the power of interest groups. These institutions helped shape the privatization of the telephone company. They help explain why the controlling shares were sold to foreigners, and the remaining shares were disseminated to the population through popular capitalism.

CONCLUSION

Although CTC performed more efficiently than most of the telephone companies in the rest of the Southern Cone. The Chilean government was able to privatize the company quickly and without opposition. It is clear that CTC's performance improved further after privatization, but this was mostly attributed to its access to new capital and not to private-sector management. The firm, however, did not face severe manipulation by major interest groups. Yet, this political factor may have been a more important factor than microeconomic performance in the privatization outcome.

At the same time, the data show that macroeconomic factors had a large impact on the Chilean privatization program. A substantial disequilibrium in the fiscal accounts drove the first privatization program, but it did not involve the sale of CTC. In fact, Chile suffered another economic crisis in 1982 without privatizing CTC. It was not until the late 1980s, when the military government felt constrained by a lack of capital and the distortions created by the large state-owned companies, that it finally sold off the telephone company. Hence, there were other factors driving the decision to privatize. It is clear that macroeconomic factors pressure governments to consider privatization as a policy option, but it is also clear that other factors ultimately affect the decision to divest state companies. In other words, poor macroeconomic conditions are a necessary but not a sufficient condition to explain the privatization phenomenon.

The political factors, however, showed the importance that strong centralized power has in executing economic policies. The Chilean national executive was extremely strong and faced very weak opposition groups. The national executive also had the discretionary power to alter institutional rules as needed; therefore, the opposition groups were not able to alter the privatization process.

NOTES

1. A subsequent investigation by a U.S. Senate subcommittee, in March 1973, found that ITT, along with the CIA, played a major role in the destabilization of Chile and the overthrow of the Allende government.

2. A group of ten Chicago-trained economists implemented the economic programs. They met weekly and eventually produced a several-hundred-page report, nicknamed *el ladrillo* (the brick), that underlined the new economic plan (Rabkin, 1994).

3. To break inflationary expectations, the government even allowed the currency to overvalue for a time (Hachette and Lüders, 1992).

4. In 1982 and 1985, CTC posted moderate losses due to changes in the exchange rate and technical problems. The latter resulted from low levels of capital investment and modernization of equipment.

5. It is important to note that CORFO was planning a fourth round of privatizations that would have involved politically sensitive companies such as CODELCO, the mining copper monopoly, and ENAMI, the state-owned copper smelter. This would have been implemented in the early 1990s, had the military government won a plebiscite to continue in power.

6. Interestingly, Brazil and other Latin American countries had accumulated their foreign debt burdens due to the overexpansion of the public sectors, whereas Chile accumulated its debt due to the unregulated and uncontrolled expansion of the private sector.

7. It is important to note that Glade (1991) argues that Chile was the only major Latin American privatization program that was not debt-related. He bases this observation on the fact that Chile did not have the state-led expansion programs seen in the other countries. Nonetheless, as we have pointed out earlier, the increased debt burden on the public sector, due to the failure of the banking system, was one of the principal drivers behind the Chilean privatization program.

8. In 1955, USAID, a U.S. development agency, launched a program to train top Latin American students in the rigors of classical economics. The agency approached the Catholic University, a highly conservative institution, and set up a program in which five students would receive scholarships each year. By the mid-1980s, the program had trained 150 Chileans. Most of the graduates returned to Chile and taught at the university or entered government. The graduates also formed CIEPLAN, a neoliberal economic think tank (*Hoy*, 1984).

9. Schneider (1992) argued that privatization in the United Kingdom and Chile was driven more by ideological factors than by economic ones—that is initiatives designed to reduce or eradicate the power of the left.

10. The military rulers had already witnessed firsthand how fiercely foreign owners would defend their property rights; for example, ITT spent over a million dollars to destabilize the Allende government (Schoenberg, 1985).

11. The decision to provide incentives to foreigners could also have stemmed from the experiences gained from the earlier privatization program. The government sold off large sections of the firms nationalized by the Allende government, thereby creating large and powerful domestic conglomerates. By the end of 1978, 5 conglomerates owned 53% of total assets of Chile's 250 largest firms, but many of these firms failed during the economic crisis of 1982 (Pietrobelli, 1994). In an effort to avoid re-

peating the mistake of concentrating too much economic power, the government may have opted to sell the companies abroad.

12. The only difference between the two types of shares is that owners of B shares can vote for the company's board of directors.

13. It is interesting to note that most of the other privatization programs in the Southern Cone were mindful of giving too much power to foreign owners and thus gave preference to local ownership.

14. The high level of organization of the copper unions may help to explain why the sector was never privatized in Chile. Furthermore, the fact that the military received 10% of copper mining (CODELCO) revenues may be a reason why the military had no incentive to divest the company (Sigmund, 1988).

15. Mayer and Meadowcroft (1986) argued that the Thatcher government wanted to maximize the dispersal of company shares. In the sale of British Telecom, 2.3 million shares were distributed. Of these shares, 4.6% went to employees, 34.4% to the public, and the rest to institutional and foreign investors.

4

URUGUAY

OVERVIEW

The analyses of the previous two cases, Telebras and CTC, revealed significant variance in microeconomic performance and privatization outcomes. However, they showed the more efficient company, CTC, was privatized, while Telebras was not. Therefore, we will proceed with the analysis of a third case, Administracion Nacional de Telecomunicaciones del Uruguay (ANTEL), to explore the interplay between microeconomic performance and privatization.

The Uruguayan case introduces a new dimension to our study of privatization. It is a case where the government received initial privatization support from all of the major and traditional political groups in the country, but was unable to win over public opinion and popular support. This chapter explores the political factors that shaped the attempt to privatize ANTEL. Specifically, it examines the role of the national executive, interest groups, and institutional rules in the privatization process.

In 1989, while Uruguay was undergoing a severe economic crisis, Luis Alberto Lacalle was elected president. He had campaigned on a platform of neoliberal economic reform and privatization. The new administration was granted a mandate to initiate a program of fundamental economic reforms. A year into his term, President Lacalle signed decrees 718 and 720, authorizing the privatization of ANTEL by the end of 1992. The Uruguayan Parliament also approved a sweeping package (*El Proyecto de Desmonopolization*) that allowed the government to restructure the economy (CERES, 1991). The privatization legislation allowed the government to sell 49% of the company; 38% would be sold to a set of qualified investors for cash, 8% would be transferred to workers, and 3% would be sold to domestic investors. Although the electorate was originally in favor of privatization, a mass publicity campaign by the public-sector unions, along with a set of crippling strikes, resulted in an overwhelming rejection of the ANTEL privatization during a referendum held in 1992, thus terminating the project.

MICROECONOMIC FACTORS

Formation and Early History

The first Uruguayan utility company providing electricity and telephone service commenced operations in 1886, and was called Compañía Telefónica y de Luz Electrica del Rio de la Plata. Despite the small size of the country and its economy, the Uruguayan government maintained a deregulated business environment to foster competition. Therefore, a host of other privately owned telephone companies, including Compañía Telefónica la Uruguaya, Compañía Telefónica de Montevideo, Sociedad Cooperativa Telefónica Nacional, and Compañía Telegráfica y Telefónica del Plata, soon emerged to provide telephone service throughout the country.

In 1915, however, Uruguay underwent a powerful political and economic transformation with the election of Jose Batlle y Ordóñez. President Batlle supported the creation of *entes autónomos* (state enterprises) to enhance the general welfare of the state, increase competition in services, and ensure international sovereignty of the country (Weinstein, 1988). These state-owned companies were granted monopoly rights by the 1917 Constitution and were authorized to absorb all of the private-sector companies in their line of business. One of the first *entes* was *Usinas Electricas y Los Telefonos del Estado (UTE),* which provided both electric and telephone service (Alisky, 1969). UTE's creation was based on the concept that monopoly rents would be used to increase investment in the network and provide telephone service to all Uruguayans. Although the two utilities operated under the same roof for over twenty years, the telephone portion of the company was separated from UTE in 1931; but it was not until July 1974 that the government formally established ANTEL. That year, Law 14325 granted ANTEL a monopoly on local, long-distance, and international telecommunications services. Unlike the Brazilian and Chilean cases, where public ownership of the telephone companies was a short-lived phenomenon, the Uruguayan case had a seventy-five-year long tradition of state ownership.

Corporate Control

As outlined in the 1917 Constitution, corporate control of the *entes* was designed to ensure political harmony and prevent drastic changes in the management staff. Article 100 of the Constitution called for plural director-ships of the firm, and this included minority representation by the opposition party. ANTEL's board of directors consisted of five individuals—three were chosen by the government in office and two were from the opposition party. During the military governments of the 1970s, however, the company structure changed slightly when it was made part of the Ministry of National Defense. Nonetheless, company operations remained relatively autonomous. The company was granted dual powers to provide telephone service and regulate itself; therefore, there was no external oversight of the firm.

Firm Performance

ANTEL has had one of the best performance records in Latin America. As shown in Table 7, the company's small size did not prevent it from providing one of the best telephone penetrations (lines per 100 inhabitants) of the four cases. Its relatively high performance explained the positive level of consumer satisfaction. In a 1992 survey, most customers considered ANTEL's telephone service to be very good (*Latin Finance*, April 1993). The company, however, had poor financial performance. One reason for the low level of revenue per line was due to low tariffs (see Table 7). Despite the low tariffs, the company managed a 15% rate of return on capital, indicating an efficient use of financial resources.

Technology

Like Chile, Uruguay never developed its own telephone equipment industry. Instead, it relied on foreign equipment manufacturers; consequently, the country was able to outfit the network with the latest technology from Europe, Japan, and North America.[1] All long-distance service was supplied by microwave links or satellite service, with surface lines used only in urban areas. In 1985, the company's management initiated a program to install fiber-optic, cellular, and digital technology in the Montevideo market. In 1989, this was updated into a four-point plan to expand and modernize the network, improve efficiency, increase competition, and integrate regional and international services. The latter two objectives allowed the establishment of foreign-owned cellular phone systems and the network's integration into global satellite communication systems, further improving the technological condition of the company. A comparison of the different levels of digitalization (Table 8) shows how the Uruguayan telephone company clearly outperformed two of the three other telephone companies. It was outperformed only by the Chilean Telephone Company (CTC), another well-managed company.

Investment and Financing

Although ANTEL's management attempted to maximize the use of scarce financial resources, the firm still suffered from a lack of capital. Due to its small size, ANTEL was excluded from international and domestic capital markets; hence, most investment capital came from self-generated revenues and government loans. One of the driving motivations to privatize the firm was to increase the level of investment. As indicated in Table 9, in 1986, ANTEL was able to invest more per line than the other three Southern Cone telephone companies; however, the company's level of investment gradually began to decline. After its 1987 privatization, CTC dramatically overshadowed ANTEL's level of investment.

Labor

Organized labor has a long tradition in Uruguay. Immigrant workers from southern Europe organized labor unions before the turn of the century. The election of President Batlle in 1915 strengthened organized labor by providing it with a powerful ally, especially since both advocated a statist type of government. While the older trade unions were traditionally based on skills and industries, modern confederations or peak associations began to emerge in 1940, with the establishment of the Unión General de Trabajadores (UGT). When the UGT was infiltrated by Communist factions during the late 1950s, a new centrist confederation, the Confederación General de Trabajo (CGT), was established (Alisky, 1969). The CGT, a more conservative group, was based on foundations similar to the Peronist labor movement in Argentina. Both advocated a strong state sector and cooperation between labor and government. Following the repression of the military period, the CGT re-emerged as the PIT–CNT, which included the workers in ANTEL.

Despite its impressive technical performance, ANTEL had the most bloated payroll, after Telebras in Brazil, in the Southern Cone. Table 10 shows that in terms of lines per employee and gross revenue per employee, the company performed very poorly. As the details of the 1992 privatization were known and it became clear that there would be a sharp reduction in the ANTEL payroll, the unions were galvanized into action. In 1992, a walkout by the company's workforce paralyzed the country's communication systems. This was followed by a seventy-two-hour general strike that brought the country to a standstill. Furthermore, a massive publicity campaign prior to the national privatization referendum warned consumers of higher tariffs, with little improvement in service. It also asked Uruguayans why they were going to give their national telephone company away when it was one of the most efficient telecommunications companies in the region.

MACROECONOMIC FACTORS

Fiscal Performance and Inflation

Uruguay's operating performance during the early 1980s was poor, in nominal terms, but representative for the region. The government suffered from high fiscal deficits, stagflation, and overwhelming debt. Many of the economic problems were attributed to the military government's focus on internal security and lavish spending on defense programs. The economic mismanagement subsided when Uruguay made a transition to civilian rule during the mid-1980s. The new civilian governments were strongly committed to reducing the fiscal deficit and bringing order to the public finances. Although they made some progress toward this goal, the trend was reversed in 1989. Political pressures from retirees led to a spike in the fiscal deficit when the government was forced to make up shortfalls in the pension fund system.[2]

In addition to funding pension obligations, Uruguay's fiscal performance was debilitated by its large public sector. State companies dominated about 30% of productive activity and controlled almost 100% of infrastructure services (World Bank, 1994). Most SOEs were very inefficient during the early 1980s. In 1982, the deficit generated by Uruguayan SOEs represented 18.4% of GDP. A modernization and investment program implemented in the late 1980s, however, increased the efficiency and operations of state companies, and by 1987 the deficit produced by SOEs comprised only 4.1% of GDP, and 1.2% by 1992. ANTEL, the state-owned telephone company, received significant levels of investment capital and was soon able to improve its operations. Thus, by the time the government attempted to sell the company, it was the best telecommunications operation in the region. In fact, ANTEL was contributing surpluses to the fiscal accounts.

A similar development occurred on the inflationary front. The Uruguayan inflation rate was relatively constant throughout the 1980s. Furthermore, it was lower than the inflation rates in most of the other nations. However, in 1990, a spike in the fiscal deficit produced a temporary resurgence of inflation. It was during this period that the Lacalle administration was elected. Subsequent government policies readjusted the fiscal balance by streamlining pension fund procedures, and by 1992 the government had cut the inflation rate by half (see Table 14). Hence, Uruguay did not suffer severe fiscal or inflationary distortions in the years of the telephone privatization attempt. Although earlier economic problems had convinced the national leadership that it needed to restructure the economy through the divestiture of state companies, by the time the Lacalle administration decided to privatize the telephone company, the crisis had passed, the economy had stabilized, and economic growth had returned (see Tables 13–15). Therefore, the sense of urgency was gone.

Foreign Debt

During the early 1980s, the military government borrowed excessively to purchase military equipment. The rise in world interest rates and the spikes in global oil prices severely strained the country's ability to meet its foreign debt obligations. As Tables 16 through 18 indicate, Uruguay had the highest debt servicing and the second highest debt level ratios in the Southern Cone. Although it tried several times to reschedule its foreign debt with creditor banks, the obligations were straining the country's thin resources. Finally, in October 1990, Uruguay reached an agreement with its creditors that provided a $267 million reduction in its public debt and a significant reduction in interest rates. The agreement, known as a Brady restructuring agreement, allowed Uruguay to substantially improve its debt servicing situation while allowing it to regain the trust of the international financial community. Therefore, like the fiscal crisis, the debt crisis was over by the time the government decided to privatize ANTEL.

Although Uruguay no longer faced a debt crisis, it still faced an unfriendly international financial market. SOEs desperately needed access to investment capital so as to continue the expansion and modernization programs; therefore, the government considered privatization as a strategic option to upgrade the country's infrastructure. Since Uruguay was not faced with an overwhelming debt crisis, it discarded the option of using debt–equity swaps in the 1991 privatization program. In other words, the new owners of companies such as ANTEL would have to pay cash for their shares in privatized companies. However, the absence of an economic crisis obscured the pressing need for privatization, and most Uruguayans saw the process as a needless divestiture of valuable state assets.

Multilateral Lending Agencies

Multilateral lending agencies played a limited role in the Uruguayan privatization process. Throughout the early 1980s, the IMF worked closely with Uruguay in helping it resolve the debt situation. The organization helped set monetary, foreign exchange reserves, and inflation goals. In 1985, Uruguay negotiated a Standby Agreement with the IMF, and it was forced to slash government spending to under 1.5% of GDP. It also initiated the set of reforms that eventually stabilized the economy later in the decade. In 1989 and 1990, the multilateral agencies provided crucial backing for the restructuring of the foreign debt. Nonetheless, as Table 19 illustrates, the IMF and World Bank did not play major roles in providing the country with assistance—this mostly came from other multilateral agencies such as the Inter-American Development Bank (IADB). The latter was mainly interested in promoting social programs, not the type of structural reforms pursued by the IMF and World Bank. Hence, the major multilateral lending organizations had little impact on the Uruguayan privatization policies (IADB, 1992).

POLITICAL FACTORS

National Executive

An analysis of the Uruguayan national executive commences with an analysis of the transition to democracy. The research on Brazil and Chile has indicated that the transitional process is a fundamental part of understanding the inherent power structure of the presidency.

Like all of the countries in the Southern Cone, Uruguay experienced a long period of authoritarian control, from 1974 to 1982.[3] The return to democracy started in September 1981, when General Gregorio Alvarez was sworn in as transitional president. Significant progress was posted for the first two years, but in 1983, negotiations with the main political parties broke down when the military refused to hold open elections. The impasse culminated in a national strike on January 18, 1984, because the military leaders refused to acquiesce, fearing that open elections would allow certain popular political factions to call for human rights trials.

In March 1984, the military government reiterated its offer to hold elections, although the conditions remained heavily circumscribed. The major political parties finally agreed, and Julio Maria Sanguinetti, of the Blancos, was elected with 38.6% of the vote: Alberto Saenz de Zumaran, of the Colorados, received 32.9%. The Frente Amplio candidate received 20.4% of the vote. President Sanguinetti took office in March 1985, only to find a vast array of economic and political problems; his first priority was democratic consolidation (McDonald, 1988).

As in Brazil, the Uruguayan presidency was intentionally weakened by the out going military regime. While the military retreated to their barracks, they remained a real, visible, and constant threat to the fragile democracy. Military leaders made very public statements, often critical, about government policies, thus limiting the national executive's free range of policy options. Furthermore, the administration's failure to wrest all political power from the military was seriously criticized by several political factions, thus undermining some of the administration's congressional support. The military threat did not recede until 1986, when the Ley Caducidad, approved by Congress, granted amnesty to the military and preventing prosecution of military leaders. With political issues absorbing most of the administration's resources and focus, it was unable to implement many economic reforms. Therefore, the overall economic situation in Uruguay continued to deteriorate throughout the late 1980s. However, national elections were looming, and it was becoming too late to commence a painful structural economic reform program.

The economy turned out to be the main issue of the 1989 presidential campaign. Luis Alberto Lacalle, of the Blancos, criticized the government's outdated statist policies and campaigned on a platform of neoliberal economic reform and privatization. Indeed, many Uruguayans voiced disappointment with the country's economic situation and expressed a need for change. Therefore, he won the election with 39% of the vote, compared with 30% for the Colorados candidate. President Lacalle, however, lacked a full and unrestrained mandate for policy change. Unlike the previous administration, which enjoyed strong party support in the Congress, the new administration faced a Congress controlled by the opposition party. During the honeymoon period following the inauguration, congressional leaders openly stated their support for the new administration's economic reforms, but their support was not unconditional—especially with regard to privatization.

Uruguay is a country with a long tradition of state-owned companies. Therefore, the sale of these companies would be highly controversial, especially among the more traditional political factions. Privatization, however, was supported by some of the more centrist factions in both political parties. Jorge Areco and Jorge Batlle, of the Colorados, negotiated a bipartisan pact with the Blancos known as the Coincidencia Nacional, that committed congressional support to the economic reform program. The new alliance established a set of three major goals for economic change: reform of the social security system, fiscal reform, and privatization of public-sector companies.[4]

Economy Minister Enrique Braga implemented a set of austerity programs to rein in some of the major economic imbalances. First, he sought to improve the social security system by rationalizing services, raising the minimum retirement age, reducing the social security agency's employment levels, and curtailing some pension benefits. Second, he addressed the fiscal situation by cutting government spending, reducing pay raises, and boosting revenues through new, temporary taxes. Third, he announced that most of the state-owned companies would be sold to the private sector. Although the reforms were necessary to reduce of the macroeconomic imbalances, the social impact of all three programs was severe. Soon, the administration's popularity began to slip in the polls; however, privatization was the program that produced the strongest reaction.

On July 15, 1990, President Lacalle sent the legislation package outlining the privatization program to the Congress. Resolution no. 1122 proposed the privatization of ANTEL and of Pluna, the national airline. Although the Congress was receptive to the idea, it was slow to approve the measure. In order to expedite the process, in January 1991 the government hired Booz Allen & Hamilton, a major international consulting firm, to assess the company's assets and design the privatization process. The Chamber of Deputies finally passed the legislation on September 27, 1991, but with some important modifications. The law, known as the Act on Public Enterprises, allowed the government to sell a concession for the operation of public services to the private sector, but it was to retain some control over the new enterprise. The Congress ordered the government to maintain a minority share in the new joint venture and a seat on the company's board of directors. Specifically, the legislation allowed the government to sell 51% of the telephone company (49% to foreign buyers and 2% going to domestic buyers). It also established a new regulatory body for the telecommunications industry.

Soon after the legislation was approved, Booz Allen & Hamilton released a report estimating the value of the firm at $1 billion. Since the government would sell only half of the company, then it would gross approximately $500 million. After paying most charges and fees, an estimated $450 million would be left. The report produced an immediate outcry from some of the members of the opposition party. While the privatization law stipulated that the proceeds be invested in social security, public health, and education, it was vague on implementation details. Some members of the opposition party were concerned that the administration would use the proceeds to enhance its standing in the upcoming national elections, especially since the privatization would occur shortly before the 1994 campaign season. Therefore, the Coincidencia Nacional began showing its first signs of strain.

Nonetheless, President Lacalle remained firmly in control of the privatization initiative. In December 1991, he appointed the Managing Director of ANTEL, Rosario Medero, to direct the privatization process. Her first step was to solicit international telephone companies to participate in the privatization process. She retained the services of Morgan Grenfel, a major investment bank, to structure the financial aspects of the deal. Medero then moved to the prequalification phase. Over forty firms expressed interest in the deal, but only eight chose to participate in the prequalification process: Telefonica de Espagña, France Telecom, STET, NYNEX, Southwestern Bell, GTE, Bell Atlantic, and Bell South; in July 1991, the government disqualified Telefonica de Espagña and STET.[5]

Although support for the economic changes was never unanimous, dissension among members of both parties was growing. The president's own vice-president, Gonzalo Aguirre, and members of his own party, led by senators Carlos Pereyra and Alberto Zumaran, were becoming vocal opponents of the privatization program. In May 1991, Health Minister Jose Alfredo Solar resigned because of his opposition to privatization. It was becoming clear that the administration's initiatives were losing some of their momentum.

On the Colorados side, an entire faction (Foro Batllista), led by former President Sanguinetti, strongly opposed the sale. Furthermore, there was growing grassroots opposition to all of the government's economic policies. The cuts in fiscal spending had successfully addressed many of the major economic problems, but they also had introduced an atmosphere of austerity. Indeed, there were already calls for a national referendum on the privatization program.[6] Early in 1992, a political alliance consisting of pensioners, leftist parties, and small factions of the opposition party failed to win the votes necessary to call a referendum, but a technicality in the law allowed for a second chance to amass the necessary votes. Once the tide of public opinion turned against the administration, it was unable to recover the initiative.

To make matters worse, it found itself facing a recalcitrant military. Although the Lacalle government did not renew the move to prosecute military leaders, it reduced of the military's size, prerogatives, and budget appropriations. Furthermore, it imposed the same controls on wages that were placed on other civil servants. In October 1992, two communiqués issued by the Centro Militar (an association of active and retired military officers) demanded salary raises. The following month, the national police went on strike, and the government was forced to acquiesce to their demands.

Therefore, the increasingly embattled administration was finding itself short of the resources needed to hold the ruling coalition together and continue with the economic reforms. The outgoing military had purposely weakened the office, and the president was unable to regain the initiative. At the same time, the interest groups opposed to the privatization program were becoming better organized and more powerful.

Interest Groups

A historical rivalry between powerful rural and urban interest groups allowed the development of a strong two-party system.[7]   Indeed, an extremely violent and bloody civil war in 1904 had left an indelible mark on Uruguayan politics. In order to prevent similar conflicts in the future, the ensuing political system provided both parties with significant guarantees and power-sharing arrangements (Weinstein, 1988). The bipolar balance also led to the development of catchall parties, which later contributed to the factionalization of the two-party system (Geddes, 1994). Both parties fractured into three major groups dispersed along the political spectrum (right, center, and left).[8] In order to provide unified party tickets in national elections, the parties often assembled intraparty coalitions from a wide assortment of political ideologies. This was the case in the 1989 campaign. Luis Lacalle, a free-market proponent, was teamed with Gonzalo Aquirre, an advocate of traditional statist policies.

The two-party system was weakened in the 1970s with the emergence of a third political party, Frente Amplio (FA). This new political group was a broad-band coalition of leftists who had defected from the main parties or had operated from outside the political system during the periods of military repression; nevertheless, they served to destabilize the power of the two main traditional parties. In the 1980s, Nuevo Espacio (NE) emerged as a similar type of organization. Although the two main parties supported Uruguay's well-established interest groups, such as trade unions and business groups, many emerging interest groups, such as disgruntled pensioners, found that the new political parties were more willing to help articulate their concerns.

One of the groups naturally opposed to the economic reforms was the unions.[9] The salary controls implemented by the Lacalle administration were especially hard for unionized workers because most of them worked in the public sector. Furthermore, the administration introduced a new set of proposals limiting the power of unions. The trade unions replied by staging five general strikes during the first six months of the administration, but infighting among labor leaders prevented the leadership of the peak labor association, PIT–CNT, from establishing a dialogue with the government (Filgueira and Papadopulos,

1994). After the administration's first year, the union's internal conflicts allowed the level of labor militancy and opposition to the privatization program to decline. Hence, the government discarded organized labor as a viable opponent to the privatization program.

As was the case in Chile, Uruguay never developed a domestic telecommunications industry. Most Uruguayan private-sector businesses were dedicated to the export of beef, hides, textiles, and wheat. These industries had steadily declined in performance and revenues since the 1950s. Therefore, they were poorly organized and relatively weak, and they did not oppose the sale of ANTEL. Nonetheless, the government sought their approval for the overall economic program. As a concession to the Camara de Industrias del Uruguay (CIU), the nation's peak business association, the government agreed to slow the pace of tariff cuts in the new Mercosur trade arrangement among the Southern Cone countries (*Latin American Weekly Report*, 1993). Indeed, the administration was able to neutralize most of the traditional bases of power, but it did not foresee the impact of the non-traditional ones. Specifically, it never anticipated that a grass-roots movements could muster the power to affect the government's policies.

The social security reforms that were implemented early in the Lacalle administration resulted in the mobilization and organization of a new and very powerful interest group consisting of retirees and pensioners (Filgueira and Papadopulos, 1994). Uruguay's social security system was one of the best-developed and best-funded pension systems in the region. Indeed, most Uruguayans saw their benefits as one of their inalienable rights. The government's reform of the system was seen as an attack. Furthermore, many pensioners saw the sale of the state companies as the dismantling of the country's most valuable assets. At local rallies, speakers denounced the government's move to divest the national patrimony and pride, especially since ANTEL was seen to be the nation's crown jewel. Last of all, the protest against the sale of ANTEL was not just against the sale of the telephone company, it was against the entire privatization program. The opposition believed that if the first privatization initiative was derailed, then the government would be unable to sell the other companies. The retirees and pensioners initially gained the traditional parties unresponsive to their pleas, but soon found support among the emerging political parties, Frente Amplio and Nuevo Espacio.

By early 1992, the growing opposition to the economic reforms and the privatization program was unraveling the Coincidencia Nacional, the ruling coalition. In January, Batllismo Radical, another faction of the Colorados, defected from the ruling group. This left only one Colorados faction in the Coincidencia, Union Colorado y Batllista; therefore, the government lost the political resources to corral and control the different groups affecting the privatization process. On October 1, 1992, the second vote on the referendum was taken, and more than the minimum 30% required of the electorate voted in favor of calling the referendum. It was set for December 1992, and Frente

Amplio mobilized a nationwide campaign to repeal the measures. This position also was backed by Foro Batllista and former President Sanguinetti.

On December 13, 1992, 78% of the electorate rejected the five critical articles of the privatization law that had been passed in October 1991. The government immediately suspended privatization of ANTEL and sought to open the issue to a nationwide dialogue. A series of nationally televised debates attempted to change the public's perception of the privatization, but it was to no avail. The opposition argued that there was no reason to privatize such a profitable company. The government countered by arguing that ANTEL lacked the necessary funds to make investments for the future, but it did not specify what investments were necessary, especially since the company already had the highest state of technology and digitalization in the region. Despite these last-ditch efforts by the government to change public opinion, the sale was shelved indefinitely.

Institutional Constraints

It is clear that Uruguay's political institutions played an important role in the attempt to privatize ANTEL. First, the structural rigidity and inflexibility of the Uruguayan political party system did not allow the incorporation of new social groups, such as pensioners and retirees. Second, the country's unusual electoral system fragmented the party and political structure, thus leading to highly divided government. The Uruguayan political system allows any party to put up several candidates. The party that wins the most votes (for all of the candidates) wins the election and the candidate within that party who secured the most votes is named president.

Gonzalez (1991) has argued that the country's double simultaneous vote—in other words, primary and runoff elections in the same process—means that the president can make no claim that he or she helped other party factions win an election. Since electoral alliances are built on expediency, and not ideology, they tend to crumble soon after the election. Furthermore, the factions within the Uruguayan political parties tend to be very divided and competitive.

Third, the country's constitutional rules allowed social movements to veto or alter major policies. The accessibility of the referendum mechanism allows groups to defeat unpopular government policies. Last, the privatization initiative was almost antithetical to the Uruguayan political system. The statist political arrangement that had been established after the 1904 civil war allowed the development of a political-economic system known as coparticipation. The system allowed both political parties to appoint members and staff to the state-owned companies, *entes* (Geddes, 1994). This arrangement ensured the sharing of power and distribution of economic rents between the two most powerful groups in the country. Therefore, the sale of the state-owned companies would lead to the breakdown of this arrangement, especially since there were still rents to be had. While many of the centrist, market-oriented factions of the parties were in favor of change, the more traditional factions, such as the Foro

Batllista of the Colorados and the Movimiento Nacional de Rocha of the Blancos, saw the change as a critical breakdown of the power-sharing arrangement.

CONCLUSION

ANTEL suffered from low levels of investment and a bloated payroll. Nonetheless, an effective management staff allowed the company to provide relatively good communication services to its clients, despite the thin resources. Furthermore, it had the highest rate of digitalization in the region and was profitable. Hence, on a company level, pressure to privatize the firm was relatively low; however, macroeconomic problems were forcing the government to consider selling state assets. Uruguay suffered from relatively serious macroeconomic problems, including a high fiscal deficit, a high rate of inflation, and a large foreign debt, but the symptoms had not yet reached crisis proportions. Hyperinflation had not ravaged the economy, nor had the country faced the form of economic breakdown that had been experienced in some of the neighboring countries. Thus, when the administration turned to privatization as a way to initiate macroeconomic reforms, it was able to negotiate political approval from the Congress, but there clearly was no common sense of urgency. This situation created an opportunity space for opposition groups to exploit and, eventually, a grassroots movement halted the sale.

Like the other cases analyzed so far, the country's leadership strongly considered the privatization option during a time of macroeconomic crisis. The desire to pursue this option was widespread enough to elect a new president committed to structural reforms; however, the passing of the crisis removed the pressure to privatize. The recovery of the Uruguayan economy in 1991 provided the opponents of the privatization initiative with the votes needed to overturn the program. Hence, it is now becoming clear that macroeconomic forces do play a major role in the privatization process. When macroeconomic conditions are negative, they create pressures for divestiture; when conditions improve, the pressure is removed. However, macroeconomic factors still do not provide a complete explanation of the privatization phenomenon.

From a political standpoint, the Uruguayan case is somewhat complex because it has a reversal in the balance of power halfway through the privatization process. It is clear that the Lacalle administration enjoyed an initial honeymoon period during which it received high levels of support from the Congress. The government, however, spent most of its honeymoon period implementing changes in the pension fund system and the fiscal situation; the privatization of the state-owned companies was a third priority. Changes in the pension fund system, however, mobilized a powerful political force consisting of pensioners who came to oppose the government on all its policies. Failure to incorporate this group into the political system allowed the government to move ahead with its policies while oblivious to the grassroots opposition movement that was growing.

As the new group's strength grew, it was able to siphon off borderline factions from the ruling coalition. It was at this time that the balance of power between the executive and interest groups swung in the opposite direction. The administration's inherent lack of support in the Congress and the fragmentation of the party system eventually left it weak, isolated, and unable to control its third policy initiative, privatization. Faced with a referendum calling for the repeal of the privatization measures, the administration attempted to expand the issue to open debate; however, it was unable to regain the initiative and the policy was shelved. Therefore, the Uruguayan case is almost a text book application of the Schattschneider model.

NOTES

1. Although Uruguay subjected its imports to high tariffs (10–45%), telephone equipment purchases made by ANTEL were exempt from all duties except a 10% port tax .

2. Uruguay's demographics have endowed it with an usually aging population; thus, the requirements of the pension fund system are unusually high. Approximately 60% of the population is economically inactive, and 17% of GDP is devoted to social security expenditures (CS First Boston, 1994a).

3. In 1972, the military waged a brutal internal war against the Tupamaros, a band of leftist guerrillas. The government granted the military forces wide powers to conduct operations. In 1973, the military took control of the government when it persuaded the elected president, Juan Maria Bordaberry, to dissolve the Congress and establish a twenty-member Council of State in its stead.

4. Uruguay has one of the most mature populations in Latin America, and this has put immense burdens on the social security system. In 1991, the system consumed 17% of GDP and 20% of the population received social security benefits (Filgueira and Papadopulos, 1994).

5. Although the government announced that the companies were disqualified for technical reasons, these were the two principal companies involved in the privatization of the Argentine telephone company. Recently there had been reports about corruption in the that process. Hence, it is believed that the government disqualified the two companies to reduce the level of controversy in the Uruguayan process.

6. The referendum became a popular vehicle of public protest in Uruguay. In April 1989, a petition was submitted requesting a referendum on the law granting amnesty to the military. While the law was upheld by 55% of the population, it set a powerful precedent that unpopular laws would be contested.

7. The rural interests who wanted a federalist type of arrangement, marked their party affiliation by white (blanco) headbands. The urban groups who wanted a republican type of arrangement, were identified by their red (colorado) headbands.

8. The Colorados' three major factions are Union Colorado y Batllista (UCB), Batllismo Radical (BR), and Foro Batllista (FB). The Blancos' three major factions are Herrerismo (H), Movimiento de Renovacion y Victoria (MRV), and Movimiento Nacional de Rocha (MNR).

9. In the late 1980s, Uruguay had 90 major trade unions, with a combined membership of 240,000, and most were concentrated in the public sector (Gargiulo, 1989).

5

ARGENTINA

OVERVIEW

The first privatization programs in Argentina were launched between 1979 and 1982, when the military government began a program of peripheral privatization. Faced with decreasing funds due to the international financial and energy crises, the government sold many secondary SOE operations. For example, most construction activities and manufacturing operations were transferred to private owners. Although the intent of the program was to increase the level of efficiency, the new firms found themselves in a monopsony market situation; hence, there were very few improvements in efficiency.

In 1982, the military government was ousted in disgrace following Argentina's defeat in the Falklands War, and the new civilian government, led by Radical president Raul Alfonsin, promised to increase the pace of privatization. Early in 1989, the Alfonsin administration announced its intent to sell the state owned telephone company, Entel, and the state airline, Aerolineas Argentinas. The Ministry of Public Works, headed by Rodolfo Teragno, lined up commitments from Spanish investors to purchase both companies. But the initiative was terminated by the Congress, which was controlled by the opposition Peronist Party. Eighteen months later, however, the new Peronist administration of President Carlos Menem divested both companies within its first nine months in office. This chapter analyzes the macroeconomic factors surrounding the two privatization attempts.

The analyses of the three previous cases have revealed the importance of micro-economic factors in understanding the forces surrounding the privatization process; however, not all the cases have followed to the expectations of the microeconomics literature on privatization. The CTC and Telebras cases contradicted the expectations, while the ANTEL case adhered to them. The results have so far been inconclusive. One pattern that is emerging, however, is that powerful interest groups, such as unions and industry groups, play a pivotal role in the process. Therefore, we move to the last case, Empresa Nacional de Telecomunicaciones (Entel).

The Argentine case is interesting because it consists of two separate observations. In October 1987, the government of Raul Alfonsin decided to sell the telephone company (Herrera, 1992). It secretly sent a delegation to the United States to see whether the Bell telephone companies would consider buying Entel. Unfortunately, there was no interest in the sale due to the political and economic situation. The U.S. companies, however, were interested in taking over as paid operators, without an equity stake. A second Argentine delegation was sent to Japan, but the Japanese telephone giant, NTT, also was not interested. Given the close-knit nature of the telecommunications industry, the German equipment manufacturer Siemens found out about the possible sale and approached the Argentine government as an interested buyer. Siemens was a major manufacturer of telephone equipment in Argentina, but the government did not want to give this foreign company such a monopoly over all telephone operations in the country. It also had very little experience in managing telephone operations.

The Alfonsin administration finally decided to approach the Spanish telephone company, Telefonica de Espagña, to sell the company. The decision to approach it was partly due to Spain's strong political support of the Alfonsin government during the transition to democracy. The company also had recently undergone a major restructuring program that had vastly improved its performance. Last of all, Spain was awash in capital. It was undertaking a massive global investment program after emerging from a strong economic expansion during the late 1980s. The rapid pace of growth following its entry into the European Community had greatly filled government coffers.

The Spanish company demonstrated a strong interest, and the Argentine government stated that it would sell a twenty-year lease for all Argentine telephone operations. In August 1987, the government announced that Entel would become Telecom, S.A. The firm would be managed by Telefonica de Espagña, and the lease would provide the operators a monopoly over the provision of all types of telecommunication services in Argentina, including cable TV but not cellular and telegraphs, for twenty-five years, with an option for an additional ten years (Senado de la Nacion, 1989). Telefonica also would gain control of the regional telephone companies. The new company would have enormous discretion in accounting standards, rules of interconnection, and definition of value-added services. The fee was $750 million for the operational control, $500 million, of which would be paid in cash ($200 million in the first year and the rest within thirty months) and $250 million in debt-equity swaps. On Monday, January 2, 1989, the Alfonsin administration presented the privatization package to the Senate; however, the program failed. A coalition consisting of the unions, the Peronist Party, and equipment manufacturers was able to gather sufficient force to defeat the proposal in Congress.[1]

In July 1989, the newly elected Peronist administration, led by Carlos Menem, launched a radical restructuring of the economy. Two weeks before entering office, he had announced the privatization of Entel. On June 24, 1989, the future Minister of Public Works, Jose Roberto Dromi, was appointed to lead the overall privatization effort along with Maria Julia Alsogaray, who was assigned as Entel's company trustee. Indeed, it was her job to carry out the sale within 180 days. Given the dire economic conditions, Alsogaray was charged with maximizing the selling price first and then ensuring competition and efficiency.

The overall privatization decree drew its powers from the State Reform Law and also modified the 1972 National Telecommunications Law, which was incompatible with privatization. On September 12, 1989, a presidential decree was signed allowing the sale of 60% of Entel to private owners through a process of competitive bidding. Of the remaining 40%, 10% would be given to the unions, and 30% would be sold at a later time to international investors through a global stock offering (Alsogaray, 1990).

To assist in the process, Alsogaray recruited Ricardo Zinn to lead the telecommunications project. She also retained the services of Morgan Stanley, a U.S. investment bank, and Price Waterhouse, a U.S. accounting firm (Petrazzini, 1993). The former would assist in designing the selling process, and the latter would help in the valuation of the company. The team from Morgan Stanley completed a study suggesting that the best way to sell the company was to break it into two units (north and south) in order to get comparative competition. Originally the company was going to be divided into seven units, then three units, but the consultants argued that it would not work. Although this type of arrangement could lead to oligopoly price-fixing by the new companies, it was the only way the government could ensure some form of competition while maximizing its selling price.

The team from Price Waterhouse worked with the National Development Bank (BANADE) and set the valuation of Entel at $3.2 billion, lower than the $3.5 billion estimated by the Alfonsin government (Alsogaray, 1990). Therefore, the 60% share to be sold would be valued at $1.92 billion. Unfortunately, valuation of the company was very difficult. Company records were almost nonexistent, and the fixed capital stock was almost obsolete. Given the poor condition of the firm, the privatization advisers suggested that the government assume the company's debts, which included $930 million in national obligations and $360 million in foreign debt, in order to make it lucrative for investors. Last of all, telephone rates were increased by 97% to make them compatible with international prices.[2]

The privatization team then decided to set the term of the exclusive franchise at seven years, with an added three years' reward if the buyer adhered to the terms of the contract. It was originally going to be for five years, but polling of the larger telecommunications companies showed that there would not be sufficient interest to bid for such a short exclusive franchise, especially since it was thought that the company would require two to three years to get it back on an even keel. Given the seven-year term and the valuation of the firm, the privatization team was able to calculate the minimum bid that would be acceptable. Since the numbers of subscribers in the northern and southern regions of the country were known, then the privatization team was able to calculate a discounted cash flow for seven years. The original base rate would provide an annual rate of return of 16%, much higher than international standards. The minimum price for the company would be $214 million in cash ($114 million for the southern unit and $100 million for the northern unit) and $380 million in bonds; the variable component would be the amount of foreign debt.

On January 5, 1990, the government finally issued the selling prospectus, known as the Pleigo, detailing the bidding schedule and process. Copies were sold for $20,000 each to fourteen potential bidders. It contained a draft of the regulatory framework, the concession outline, the tariff structure, the operational requirements, and the bidding process (Dromi, 1991). Bidders had to prove that they were providers of telecommunication services with total assets in excess of $4 billion and liquid assets of $1 billion. Last of all, the Pleigo set the bidding date as April 19, 1990, with a contract date of August 6, and transfer in October. Of the fourteen potential bidders, only seven requested to be prequalified: Cable and Wireless, NYNEX, Telefonica, STET, GTE, France Telecom, and Bell Atlantic.

Prequalified bidders were allowed to inspect the company books and facilities during the period between the issuance of the Pleigo and the bidding date. Most of them sent teams down to assess the company's condition. However, changes in the Pliego would sour the mood. Several members of Congress accused the government of selling the company too cheaply, pointing out that the 1988 valuation of the firm was $3.5 billion, but now it was $3.2 billion. On March 28, 1990, the administration responded by raising the company valuation to $3.5 billion, thus elevating the minimum bids. Responding to pressure from the public, on April 11, the Congress demanded that the government reduce the base rate. It also demanded a reduction in the prerequisite total assets for qualified operators from $1 billion to $1.5 billion. This would increase the possibility of local groups' participating in the bidding process. Faced with such constant changes in the bidding environment, several prequalified bidders dropped out.

By the bidding date, only three bidders tendered offers for the two regions. Since the amount of tendered debt was the only variable that would be examined, the bid analysis was short. When the bids were disclosed, the winning offers for both north and south were from Telefonica, a consortium that included Citibank and Techint, an Argentine industrial conglomerate. Since it could be awarded only one of the regions, it chose the southern region because it was the more populous.

The northern region was awarded to the Bell Atlantic consortium, which included Manufacturers Hanover Trust, which came in second place. The third and losing consortium was the Italian–French consortium of STET and France Telecom. They allied with J.P. Morgan and Perez Companc. U.S. law, however, prevented any of the U.S. Bell telephone companies from owning more than 4.9% of a foreign telephone operator. Hence, the Pleigo had to be changed accordingly. As the transfer date approached, the Bell Atlantic consortium announced to the government that its investment bank, Manufacturers Hanover Trust, was having difficulty in amassing the needed debt instruments. The government gave the team thirty additional days, but it was still unable to resolve the situation. Public Works Minister Dromi and Entel Trustee Alsogaray feuded over the situation. While Alsogaray wanted to give preference to the American telephone companies, STET and France Telecom expressed their desire to buy the northern unit. Italy and Argentina had recently signed a bilateral agreement that gave the Menem government $5.5 billion in economic aid. Italian Ambassador De Michelis also had announced that Argentina would be given a $135 million loan for the improvement of the Buenos Aires phone system—provided that 90% of the contracts went to Italcable and Telettra. Hence, Dromi was anxious to please the Italians. Alsogaray favored Bell Atlantic because it possessed U.S. technology, which was seen as superior to European technology. Furthermore, management of the Entel by one the U.S. Bells would be prestigious for Argentina. Finally on October 4, President Menem announced that he would not provide Bell Atlantic with additional time. The STET-France Telecom consortium was allowed to bid, and it matched the Bell Atlantic offer. Hence, it was able to complete the process by November 1990.

It is clear that although the Peronists opposed the 1988 privatization attempt, they were able to successfully divest the company in less than six months. The next section examines the microeconomic conditions of the company to understand how they impacted the process.

MICROECONOMIC FACTORS

Formation and Early History

Telephone service in Argentina was first established in 1880, with the formation of the Sociedad de Pantelephone de Loch in Buenos Aires. Shortly thereafter, two more companies entered the market—Gower Bell and Continental de Telefonos Bell. In 1886, a merger of the three companies under British management created Union Telefonica de Rio de la Plata (UTRP); however, prices rose after the first year of operation, while service declined. In 1887, a group of consumers, upset with the poor service and high prices, created the Sociedad Cooperativa Telefonica (SCT) to provide an alternative telephone company. SCT launched operations with 1,000 customers, whereas UTRP had 7,000, but it eventually became the largest telephone operator in Argentina by offering similar services at lower prices (Petrazzini, 1993).

In 1925, the Telephone Company of New York , which later became ITT, injected a capital infusion into SCT when the latter began facing financial problems. Two years later, ITT increased its investment and purchased all of SCT's 195,000 lines. The deal was consummated with the assistance of J.P. Morgan, a U.S. investment bank, and became part of an arrangement demarcating the global telecommunications market.[3] In 1929, ITT established a monopoly over all telephone service in Argentina by purchasing the shares of UTRP. The multinational's monopoly provided Argentine consumers with good service until World War II, when the network entered a period of decay due to a lack of new equipment and replacement parts.

After the war, Argentina found itself in the unusual situation of possessing large quantities of almost useless British currency that had accumulated from the sale of wheat and beef during the war. The money had limited value because the British Parliament passed a nonconvertibility law, thus restricting Argentina's range of options. Therefore, the government of Juan Peron engineered a plan to purchase British and other foreign-owned assets located in Argentina with the currency. The government acquired the ports, railroads, electric utilities, and subways, and on September 3, 1946, it purchased the telephone company for £28 million (Petrazzini, 1993). To provide for a smooth transition, ITT was paid a fee to manage operations until Argentine managers could be trained.[4]

The name of the new state company was changed several times during its early history. First it was Empresa Mixta Telefonica Argentina; later it became Direccion Nacional de Telefonos del Estado; and finally in 1956, it took on the name Entel. Unlike the telephone companies in Chile and Brazil, Entel provided both urban and long-distance service under the same organization; however, Entel only had 92% of the Argentine market. Another telephone company, Compania Argentina de Telephonos, S.A. (CAT), provided services to six of the largest provinces: Mendoza, San Juan, Santiago del Estero, Salta, Tucuman, and Entre Rios.

CAT was once a domestically owned telephone company, but it was absorbed by the Swedish equipment manufacturer L.M. Ericsson Telephone Company in 1936, after the Argentine company defaulted on equipment loans. Ericsson wanted to sell CAT to the Peron government when UTRP was nationalized, but it demanded an amount equal to what was paid to ITT. The government had almost completed the transaction when President Peron was overthrown by a coup in 1955. The government then issued a decree prohibiting CAT from investing in the network until an arrangement could be negotiated, but in 1959, President Arturo Frondizi decided not to buy the company. CAT was allowed to raise rates and expand its network. In 1989, CAT services comprised 7% of the market, and the remaining 1% was provided by 165 small cooperatives that served rural areas.

Political Control

Of the four companies examined, Entel experienced the most political control and interference. The firm's management reported to the Ministry of Public Works, and managers were appointed by the political leadership. Unfortunately, the management experienced high rates of turnover due to the instability of Argentine governments. Starting in the late 1950s, and over a period of twenty-five years, Entel had twenty-eight different executive directors, and the average tenure for company directors was nine months (Petrazzini, 1993). Between March 1984 and October 1987, Argentina had four ministers of public works, four secretaries of communications, and three administrators of Entel. In addition to inconsistent management, the company suffered from diffuse control. The Ministry of the Economy produced Entel's budget, the Ministry of Labor set salaries, and the Secretariat of Industry decided on equipment purchases. Political appointees directed most strategic and operational activities, while the professional staff was delegated to functionary tasks (Herrera, 1989).

Firm Performance

Although Argentina had the second largest telephone network in the Southern Cone, its performance was poor. Waiting time for installation of new telephone service averaged fourteen years, and the completion rate for telephone calls was 42%. Entel, however, did have the second highest penetration rate (lines per 100) in the region and, in 1986, it collected the highest revenue per line. Nonetheless, performance decreased consistently until after the privatization of the company in 1989, when it finally began to recover (see Table 7).

Technology

Fortunately, Entel did not follow Brazil's example and develop its own technology standards. It, however, did implement inconsistent and, often, incoherent technology plans. Most of these inconsistencies were attributed to the rapid turnover in management and a highly politicized decision making body. For example, a decision in 1985 to upgrade the network with new digital technology led to the acquisition of the equipment and lines; however, no measures were taken to integrate the new format with the forty year-old equipment that was already in place. The results were a drastic decay in telephone service and cost overruns while the problem was resolved. By the time the company was privatized, the Entel network consisted of seven different technological formats, most of them almost incompatible with each other.

The result of poor technological policies led to severe bottlenecks and delays in the modernization of the system. As Table 8 shows, Entel's level of digitalization significantly lagged all of the other networks in the region. In fact, the network was in such bad shape that many businesses created their own private networks, thus strewing the Buenos Aires skyline with wires hanging between buildings. Some large companies even built their own microwave towers. Large multinational corporations, such as, IBM, Citibank, and American Express, installed privately owned satellite communication networks. This by-pass of Entel caused an approximate $200 million loss each year.

Investment and Financing

The highly politicized control of Entel produced erratic patterns of investment. For example, in 1975 the company purchased 6,000 new telephone lines, and four years later it increased procurement by 3,300% to 200,000 new lines (Herrera, 1992). Such erratic changes required adjustments in manpower, planning, and infrastructure, which Entel failed to do. Each dramatic increase in investment was accompanied by an equally dramatic reduction soon thereafter. In 1988, the government repeated the pattern when it implemented the Megatel Plan.[5] Since there was such a large backlog of potential customers, applicants wanting a new telephone line were asked to pay $1,000 in advance. The installation fee was to be used for the purchase of the new equipment. Approximately 600,000 new customers immediately signed up, but failure to account for the surge in related costs, as well as a spike in inflation, sabotaged the plan. Megatel was a public relations disaster for the government. Failure to record the payment of deposits forced the government to send out notices that new subscribers would not receive telephone service if they could not prove that they had paid their deposits. Furthermore, since the fees were collected in australs, the hyper-inflationary environment significantly eroded the new capital infusion.

Entel also suffered from erratic pricing schemes. Like other telephone companies, it cross-subsidized urban rates with long-distance rates. However, there was such an imbalance between the two that urban rates did not cover costs of operations or investment. Furthermore, politicized pricing schemes severely undermined the company's revenue base. For example, most government ministries were exempt from paying for telephone service and retired individuals were granted service that was virtually free.

Equipment Manufacturing and Purchasing

Argentina implemented an import-substitution industrialization (ISI) program during the 1970s in order to develop a domestic telecommunications equipment industry. However, it did not decide to establish its own technological standards, though the creation of the ISI program eventually led to the formation of politically powerful industrial groups. The major industrial associations were Grupo Maria, Union Industrial de Argentina (UIA), Camarra Argentina del Commercio (CAC) and Consejo Empresario Argentino (CEA) (Smith, 1991). These were large industrial groups that could compete in the international market, but they also provided goods and services to state-owned enterprises as the ISI policies of the 1970s accelerated. The smaller firms that were dedicated suppliers to the state companies were represented by the Confederacion General de Economica (CGE) and the Confederacion General de Industria (CGI) (Acuña, 1993a).

The establishment of a domestic telephone equipment industry was designed to prevent the shortages that occurred during the world wars, but it also led to the establishment of strict, politically mandated acquisition rules that forced the company to pay extremely high prices for domestically manufactured equipment and services. The Regimen de Compre Nacional, enacted by President Arturo Illia, granted preferential status to domestic companies bidding for government contracts (Herrera, 1992). The law required all SOEs to purchase materials and services from domestic sources, as long as it did not impede the technology transfer.[6]

The development of a domestic equipment manufacturing industry spawned powerful interest groups that eventually controlled the telephone company. These firms included Siemens, Equitel, NEC, Alcatel, and Telettra (Herrera, 1989). Not only were these firms developed to provide telecommunications equipment to the Argentine market, but they were also part of a global expansion of telecommunications equipment manufacturers that occurred in the late 1970s and early 1980s. European telecommunications firms were especially aggressive in pushing into the Argentine market.[7] They were followed by the U.S. Bell companies and the Japanese manufacturing firms (Herrera and Petrazzini, 1992).

The German telecommunications equipment manufacturing firm Siemens had a long presence in Argentina. It had provided most of the technology for Entel and was owed $500 million by the Argentine government (Siemens, 1992). This was one of the chief reasons that it wanted to buy Entel; thus, it could apply its $500 million credit to the sale (*Apertura*, 1990). The country's commitment to ISI policies and the strong inflow of capital allowed the emergence of a new group of industrial conglomerates that provided a wide range of products and services to state-owned enterprises. Whenever a domestic firm lacked a specific technology, a joint venture with a foreign firm was established. This was definitely the case in the mid-1980s when Entel decided to acquire digital technology.

Perez Companc, a powerful government supplier, established a joint venture with NEC, a Japanese manufacturing firm, to build digital equipment in Argentina. The new firm, called Pecom-NEC, forced Entel to acquire the equipment from it—albeit at 300% over international prices. In 1986, Techint S.A, another Argentine conglomerate, formed a similar joint venture with Telettra and Italcable, two Italian equipment manufacturers. The company was already heavily involved in construction projects for Entel, and this venture provided it with an entry into telecommunications equipment manufacturing. By the late 1980s, the major suppliers were Siemens of Argentina and Pecom-NEC; and by the time of the privatization, the state-owned telephone company owed these firms over $1.2 billion.

Other firms included Alactel, the equipment manufacturing arm of France Telecom, one of the eventual owners of Entel, which offered the Argentine government low-interest loans to set up manufacturing plants for the local market (Herrera, 1989). These domestic firms not only possessed power over Entel operations, but they also had an indirect financial hold on the company. Equipment debts owed by Entel to the manufacturers were held as bargaining tools. The power of these firms was clearly exposed when they vetoed the first privatization attempt. Under the 1988 privatization plan, the domestic manufacturing firms were not a party to the new ownership structure. Indeed, they would lose their access to the exclusive, and lucrative, equipment manufacturing markets. Under the second privatization plan, not only did large local groups, such as Bridas, Perez Companc, and Techint, become partial owners of the newly privatized companies, but the large European telecommunication equipment manufacturing firms captured a lucrative new client for their products.

Labor

Entel had a large, well-organized, and militant workforce. Of the 48,000 employees, 98% belonged to one of the three telecommunications labor federations, FOETRA, FEJEPROC, and FOECYT. There was a large concentration of the unionized workforce in Buenos Aires, where 27,000 of the 48,000 members resided. The labor performance statistics (see Table 10) reveal a good, but inconsistent, implementation of labor. On a revenue per employee and line per employee basis, the company often performed better than the other companies in the region, but the trends were never consistent. This, however, was attributed to erratic management decisions on expansion, tariffs, and policies. For example, the 1988 Megatel plan greatly expanded the network and increased revenues, but it failed to augment the increase in lines with a corresponding increase in technicians; thus it increased the work for existing staff and created backlogs (Hill and Abdala, 1993).

While the union leaders were not able to alter the situation in staffing levels, they did play a pivotal role in both attempts to privatize Entel. The first began with the union leadership strongly opposed to the national administration. President Raul Alfonsin, of the Radical Party, had reduced relations with organized labor to open conflict because his administration attempted to democratize labor and replace union bosses. Since his election in 1983, President Alfonsin had attempted to remove the vestiges of authoritarianism in Argentina and reestablish democracy (Acuña, 1993b). The national confederation of workers (CGT) was the most prominent labor federation and a pillar of political power in Argentina, but since the administration of Juan Peron, it had also become a bastion of Peronist power. Alfonsin's measures tried to dismantle the link between the party and the union's structure, but it only provided a catalyst that brought together the two factions of the CGT: CGT-Azopardo, headed by Jorge Triaca, and CGT-RA, headed Saul Ubaldini.[8] The truce between the two camps was uneasy and there were clear lines of division between them. However, the new union hierarchy was vehemently opposed to President Alfonsin's measures. The unified CGT allied itself with the industrial groups, such as the CGE, and launched a series of thirteen devastating strikes that paralyzed Argentina for weeks.

The second privatization attempt occurred in a different labor environment. The militant CGT labor leader, Saul Ubaldini, joined Menem's team during the election. With the election of Menem, a Peronist, as president, the unions had an ally in office. Although his decision to privatize the telephone company came as a shock, the CGT could not unify against the administration's policies. The unionized workforce did not know how to react when the administration issued Decree 731, which transferred 45,000 Entel employees from state employment to the private sector. Of those transferred, 21,500 went to the southern telephone unit, 19,002 to northern telephone unit, 630 to Startel, and 1,506 to Telintar. President Menem then turned against Ubaldini, giving the position of Minister of Labor went to his rival, Jorge Triaca.

The CGT leadership immediately called for a caucus of the federations. Unable to come to terms on the issue, the CGT again broke into two factions. The Menem loyalists departed the CGT offices and reconvened at the San Martin Theater. They mostly represented workers from private–sector unions, except those from the rail unions, which had already pledged to support Menem's privatization of the national railroad. This group became known as the CGT-San Martin. The other was CGT-Azopardo. President Menem recognized CGT-San Martin as the only legal representative of workers and rewarded its leaders by allowing them lucrative concessions such as full discretion in the management of their welfare and social funds. The other unions faced harsh repression. For the first time in decades, the government began dismissing workers who participated in strikes regarded as illegal, such as those in the telephone, rail and oil industries. An attempt by CGT-Azopardo to stage a devastating twenty-four-hour strike failed due to low cooperation and poor turnout. Furthermore, attempts to ally itself with industrial groups providing ISI goods and services were fruitless. The new privatization rules required participation by local business interests, thus guaranteeing them partial ownership of the new privatized telephone company.

MACROECONOMIC FACTORS

Fiscal Performance and Inflation

The section on microeconomic factors provided an in-depth analysis of the development of the public sector in Argentina. Using the case of Entel, it illustrated the dramatic expansion of state-owned enterprises during the 1940s and 1950s, under the guidance of Juan Peron . The acquisitions made by Peron were conducted with foreign exchange reserves that had accumulated during World War II and surpluses produced by the agricultural sector. The agricultural sector also contributed a considerable share of the surpluses that were used to subsidize the industrial expansion in the post war years (Waisman, 1990). But the bloated state sector soon introduced distortions into the Argentine economy and created a growing disequilibrium in the fiscal accounts (Diaz-Alejandro, 1970). However, it was not until the 1970s that the damage caused by the expansionist programs finally became apparent; the inflation rate grew to 300% and government deficit spending increased to 15.5% of GDP.

Most of the fiscal imbalance was generated by the large subsidies that were provided to state-owned enterprises and the inefficient system of tax collection. In 1989, losses from state-owned companies reached $5.5 billion.

Gerchunoff (1993) noted that the balance sheets of the majority of the state-owned companies reached crisis proportions by 1988. Indeed, three state companies–telephone, railways, and oil—accounted for 50% of the losses. They also generated a large portion of the country's debt. Between December

1989 and December 1990, Entel's debt rose from $1.29 billion to $2.14 billion (Petrazzini, 1993).

Argentina placed itself in an even more precarious position because it financed a large portion of the public deficit through foreign debts and increases in the money supply (Gershunoff, 1993). In 1983, the new civilian economic team attempted to address the growing macroeconomic problems, but the administration's first priority was political reconciliation following the long period of military dictatorship. Economy Minister Bernardo Grinspun made a subtle attempt to solve the economic crisis through a heterodox stabilization program (Cardoso and Helwege, 1992). This included the use of price controls and higher levels of public spending while raising government revenues through increased taxes on exports.

The new measures increased revenues by 18.6%, but the government was not able to make much progress on reducing the level of fiscal spending. Since the budgetary process was based on bilateral negotiations with special interest groups, the new and fragile civilian government was limited in enforcing strict economic rules or gaining concessions from groups. Therefore, the macroeconomic situation continued to deteriorate due to the inherent economic problems. Furthermore, the use of price controls and export taxes prevented the adjustment of prices, and export taxes reduced the competitiveness of Argentine products.[9]

It is no surprise, then, that the economic stabilization program failed and the administration was forced to appoint a new economy minister, Juan Sourrouille. In June 1985, the new economic team introduced the Austral Plan to stabilize the economy. The plan expanded wage and price controls and froze the exchange rate. In the short term, it brought stability to the country and allowed the fiscal balance to improve. Inflation fell to 82% year-on-year in 1986, the lowest level in twelve years, the deficit decreased to 4.1% of GDP; and the economy expanded by 5.7% (Canitrot and Sigal, 1992).

Nonetheless, the Austral Plan had inherent flaws. Instead of using the level of orthodoxy found in most IMF-sanctioned stabilization plans, it attempted to induce stabilization without any pain.[10] Heterodox plans usually give the appearance of stability in the short term, but the removal of price controls almost always results in the revival of inflation. Indeed, this was the case in 1986, when the government liberalized prices. The exponential spike in prices forced the government to reinstate price controls immediately (see Tables 15 and 17); hence, underlining the inherent flaws of the economic plan.[11]

In August 1988, the government launched the Spring Plan, its last attempt at stabilizing the economy. This time the plan was more market-oriented. It was designed to boost the economy by May 15, 1989, the time frame of the upcoming national elections. However, most economic and social actors had lost confidence in the administration's ability to manage the economy, and Argentina plunged into a deep recession. With the fiscal deficit registering an incredible 21.8% of GDP, the government finances were in complete shambles (see Table 13). It was during this period that the government decided to privatize Entel.

Telefonica de Espagña, the Spanish state-owned telephone company, agreed to pay $1.2 billion for a 40% stake in the Argentine telephone company. The privatization was seen as an emergency measure that would provide the government with much-needed revenues to address the fiscal and debt crises. The project was sent to the Congress for approval, but the growing distrust of the Alfonsin administration resulted in its rejection. Hence, the administration was left with no other alternatives. Finally, in February 1989, the social fabric broke down. The Central Bank was forced to declare a bank holiday and suspended all foreign exchange operations. The result was devastating. The austral plummeted, inflation doubled, and prices took off. Business groups openly declared their opposition to the government's economic programs, and the World Bank immediately suspended a $350 million disbursement of credits.

The economic breakdown coincided with the 1989 national elections, and even the Radicals' own candidates disavowed the economic program. In fact, the Radical presidential candidate, Eduardo Angeloz, called for the resignation of the entire economic team. By July 1989, the economy was suffering from the onslaught of hyperinflation. Wholesale and retail prices went up 200% in a single month, and consumer prices surged 3,079% for the year. Thus, it was little surprise that the Radical party was voted out of office by an overwhelming margin and that the Peronists took control of the government.

The newly elected administration, led by Carlos Menem, initiated a program to stabilize prices, reduce public debt, and improve relations with external creditors. The first economic team was led by Miguel Roig, a senior executive from Bunge y Born (Acuña, 1993a). Bunge y Born was a powerful food export conglomerate that had traditionally opposed the government's statist and protectionist policies. The appointment of Roig was one of the first signals that the new administration would break with traditional Peronist economic policies and shift to more market-oriented ones. Unfortunately, Roig was in office for six days before he died on July 14,1989. He was immediately replaced by Nestor Rapanelli, the general manager of Bunge y Born. Rapanelli moved ahead with the implementation of key legislation packages to restore economic stability. The measures were briefly successful. Consumer prices fell from 196.6% in July to 38.0% in August, and 5.6% in October (Acuña, 1993a).

The first legislation package was the State Reform Law, which was passed on August 17, 1989. It was a sweeping set of economic initiatives that allowed the privatization of 32 of the 400 state-owned companies, and authorized the executive branch to place trustees in charge of all state companies for 180 days. The second important legislation package was the Law of Economic Emergency. It was passed on September 1, 1989, and gave the president the right to suspend subsidies to state-owned enterprises, industrial promotion subsidies, and tax breaks. Indeed, Petrecolla, Porto, and Gerchunoff (1992) argued that one of the key motives for the Argentine privatization program was the reduction of the fiscal deficit. Through selling state-owned companies, the government would be able to stabilize the economy by reducing much of its capacity to redistribute income.

The president also called for immediate privatization of Entel and Aerolineas Argentina, stabilized the currency, and brought some equilibrium to the fiscal balance by raising rates on public services by 20% to 80% and increasing export taxes by 11%, thus putting downward pressure on inflation. Unfortunately, Rapanelli's economic program became controversial within his own company, Bunge y Born. The stabilization of the austral, coupled with a high residual rate of inflation, led to an overvaluation of the currency, thus hurting exporters. Hence, Bunge y Born put pressure on the government to devalue the currency. In November 1989, the administration allowed a 54% devaluation of the austral and inflation rose again—prices surged 40% in one month. By December 1989, Rapanelli was forced to resign and was replaced by Antonio Erman Gonzalez, a former economy minister from the province of La Rioja (Acuña, 1993b).

The new economy minister launched a stabilization plan that included another devaluation of the austral, fixing of the exchange rate, imposition of wage and price controls, and a sharp increase in public utility rates. These measures managed to bring monthly inflation down to 7%, but the continued use of price controls indicated that hyperinflation would soon return. As a result, the austral declined sharply. Indeed, during December the currency plunged from 960 australs per dollar to 2,000 australs per dollar. By March 1990, annualized inflation reached 20,594%. Hence, the government was forced to abandon the economic plan.

In late 1989, the government announced the Bonex Plan. The new, IMF-approved stabilization plan abandoned wage, price, and exchange controls. Instead, it liberalized prices and launched new initiatives to restrain the public deficit—the principal cause of Argentina's chronic inflation. The plan allowed the government to convert approximately $1.5 billion in privately held bank deposits into long-term dollar debt. The result was a sharp decline in the money supply, and the country plunged into a deep recession. In order to implement further fiscal balance, the government restricted the lending activities of public-sector banks.

Unfortunately, 1990 was not much better for Argentina. Despite some of the fiscal reforms implemented by the administration, a severe deterioration of the social security system and the poor finances of the provincial governments again led to an overexpansion of Central Bank credits.[12] The economic team mounted a rescue of the social security system that allowed it to meet its year-end obligations. Furthermore, mandated cuts in spending by the provincial governments decreased their deficits, but the fiscal imbalance put more downward pressure on the austral. Finally, in 1991, Gonzalez resigned and was replaced by Foreign Minister Domingo Cavallo, a Harvard Ph.D. in economics. The new economic team finally put the economy on an even keel by drastically reducing the public-sector deficit, adjusting prices, raising taxes, and replacing the currency (peso).

Foreign Debt

Debt crises are nothing new for Argentina. It has experienced several external payment emergencies since the 1800s.[13]   In 1983, when President Alfonsin took office, the external debt stood at $45 billion, double the level of the late 1970s. This was largely a result of the A-251 Program that converted private-sector debt into public-sector debt. It also included $12 billion of Entel debt for equipment purchases. By the early 1980s the debt situation began to take on crisis proportions.

In August 1982, the Mexican moratorium on debt and the Malvinas War had led to suspension of additional credit by foreign lending institutions. Faced with an accelerating crisis, the Argentine government was forced to assume foreign obligations held by private and public companies (Canitrot and Sigal, 1992). However, the country continued to need money to service its foreign trade obligations. Hence, the advisory committee of creditor banks provided the country with additional funds. The IMF and World Bank also assisted by approving a Paris Club restructuring of the official debt obligations. However, the Radical government soon adopted a policy of debt repudiation. With foreign debt obligations reaching 107% of GDP (see Table 17), the position of the civilian government was that the debts were obligations of an illegal military government and were not the responsibility of the current administration.

The government's position, however, was ignored by the international financial community. It wanted immediate repayment of the debt and refused to provide additional credit until the matter was settled. The denial of foreign credit was devastating for Argentina. With a low level of domestic savings, it lacked the capital resources for investment and growth. This situation became clearly evident in the decision to pursue the Megatel Plan. As described earlier, the plan allowed subscribers to purchase telephone lines in advance, thus providing the government with capital to invest in the equipment.

In 1988, the debt crisis worsened when the balance of payments deficit widened to $1.4 billion and interest payments on commercial bank debt went into arrears. Faced with ever-increasing debt (see Table 19) due to international interest rates, penalties, and arrears, the government finally suspended all payments to the creditor banks in April. The government was desperate for short-term revenue, so it turned to the sale of the telephone company and the airline. The proposed sale of the telephone company included $250 million in debt-equity swaps. Since debt was trading at a discounted price of $0.12 per dollar, this meant that the Argentine government could retire over $2 billion in debt; nevertheless, the Peronist-led Congress flatly rejected the privatization option. However, debt would play a pivotal role in the second attempted sale of Entel.

Maria Julia Alsogaray, the trustee assigned to sell the telephone company, was ordered to maximize the amount of debt that would be canceled through its sale. But the debt-equity swap approach she used was slightly different from that used in other programs. It required debt cancellation, which meant that bidders had to provide the entire debt instrument, interest coupons, and arrears. This required the interested parties to build large consortia of bidders that held the diverse paper. Entel was purchased by a consortium of thirty-five corporations, more than 83% of which were financial institutions. Many of the bidding teams that lost were unable to amass the necessary debt instruments. Although the Telefonica bid of $2.720 billion in debt paper and the STET bid of $2.308 billion seem much larger than the original $1.9 billion combined bid that was required, if the debt paper is marked to market prices at the time, the bids are equivalent to $416 million and $353 million. Nonetheless, the government was happy to erase that debt from its books.

Multilateral Lending Agencies

Although Argentina has often had periods of poor relations with the major multilateral lending agencies, its overall relationship has been positive. This is clearly illustrated in Table 19, which shows that the country had strong capital inflows from the multilateral agencies up to 1989. But in 1988, the government allowed the IMF and World Bank programs to lapse, and payments to both agencies were delayed. Furthermore, the gross economic mismanagement that occurred from 1989 to 1990 resulted in a suspension of multilateral funds (Armijo, 1994).

Faced with a growing crisis, the IMF and World Bank delayed the delivery of crucial funds, which pushed the country even closer to the precipice of economic breakdown. Furthermore, the IMF's refusal to back the Alfonsin administration's last stabilization plan, the Spring Plan, was tantamount to a vote of no confidence (Damill and Frenkel, 1990). However, the new Menem administration had a response from the multilateral lending organizations. Even though Carlos Menem had campaigned on a platform of debt repudiation, the multilateral lending organizations were very receptive to his proposals. Once he was inaugurated in 1989, the new government accommodated the multilateral lending agencies by launching an IMF-sanctioned stabilization plan, *Reforma del Estado*. The response from the multilaterals was immediate;

within a month, the IMF approved a new $150 million package. Therefore, the multilateral agencies played a significant role in guiding Argentina toward privatization.[14]

POLITICAL FACTORS

National Executive

As in the other Latin American countries, the Argentine transition to democracy provides an important insight into the power of the national executive. Although Argentina had established a long tradition of democratic rule from the latter half of the 1800s to the first quarter of the 1900s, the breakdown of civilian rule in 1930 and the eventual reign of Juan Peron severely undermined the country's democratic traditions. Military governments controlled the country during most of 1955–1982; however, the military forces began disintegrating in the 1970s. During the 1970s, the military repression of leftists and subversive groups led to a decline in morale and professionalism. The proliferation of death squads, each with a secret leader, eventually destroyed the military's chain of command (Acuña and Smulovitz, 1993).

By 1979, the General Staff was no longer in control of the military. However, it was not until the humiliating rout of the Argentine expeditionary forces during the Malvinas War that the military regime dissolved. This event finally broke its remaining solidarity and allowed the return of democratic rule.[15] Therefore, unlike other Latin American countries, where the military played a major role in negotiating the transition to democracy, the Argentine military was forced to accept whatever terms were dictated by the new civilian government. At first glance this should have created an opportunity for that government to consolidate its position, but this situation also opened an opportunity for open competition and bidding by the plethora of Argentine social, economic, and political groups.[16]

The opening of the political system witnessed the return of the two traditional Argentine political parties, the Radical and the Peronists. National elections were held in October 1983, and Raul Alfonsin of the Radical Party won with 51.7% of the vote. The national elections, however, resulted in a divided government. While the Radical Party controlled the presidency and the Chamber of Deputies, the Peronists controlled the Senate.[17] This situation would result in many political stalemates.

Soon after inauguration, the new administration faced two major problems. First, there was the deteriorating economic situation; second there was the need to consolidate the newly established democracy. Bounded by limited resources and capacities, the Alfonsin government chose to tackle the latter. Waisman (1990) argued that the political obstacles to the consolidation of democracy appeared more daunting than the economic ones; yet, ironically, it was the economic situation that eventually brought down the Alfonsin government. Along the same lines, Canitrot and Sigal (1992) noted that the new civilian administration was convinced that the economic problems were the product of the inept military government, and that the international financial community would not hold the current government accountable for debts accumulated by the illegal military rulers. Hence, the administration thought that it had the freedom of movement to focus only on the country's political problems.[18] In order to consolidate the re-established democracy, the government developed a twofold strategy. First, it would limit the power of the military, and then it would curtail power of the Peronist party.

The Alfonsin administration's method of restraining the military's power was to prosecute the military officers who were involved in human rights violations during the repression of the 1970s and 1980s. Top military officers were tried and convicted in highly publicized court proceedings, almost reminiscent of the Nuremberg trials. While the trials were supposed to be limited to only the top officers, the judges' zeal expanded the prosecution proceedings to all military officers and personnel (Acuña and Smulovitz, 1993). The proceedings became show trials and the process showed no sign of abating. The military officers, however, could take only so much humiliation before striking back.

In April 1987, Lieutenant Colonel Rico led the first of a series of military coups that sought to overthrow the government. Although this rebellion was put down, two more uprisings within six months were led by other members of the officer corps (Canitrot and Sigal, 1992). The revolts did not seek a return to military rule, each demanded the granting of general amnesty. Unfortunately, each revolt drained the administration's limited resources, and by 1989, many Argentine analysts felt that the government would not be able to put down another revolt.

The administration's second political priority was to destroy the Peronist Party's power structure. There was a perception among many Argentine intellectuals that its domination of the country's political system since the 1930s had led to subsequent authoritarian regimes. Indeed, Peronism was initially an authoritarian type of political arrangement that had been subsequently taken on democratic trappings. Since most of the party's power was centered in the strong links between the party and the unions, members of the Radical Party attempted to reduce the power of the party by removing some of these formal and legal ties. The Alfonsin administration drafted a new labor legislation package to democratize the internal decision-making mechanisms of the large labor organizations; however, this proved to be a poorly timed tactic.

Although the Peronist Party and the unions had emerged from the military period in a state of disarray, they had been shocked by the defeat of the Peronist Party during the 1984 national elections. Indeed, the defeat was interpreted by Peronists as a strong vote of no confidence by the Argentine population (Canitrot and Sigal, 1992). Now the party and unions were going to be ripped apart by the government, a perception that galvanized both into action. The initiative served as a catalyst for the party to reorganize the union and party leadership, and consolidate their structures. The only way the Peronists could defeat the legislation package was through the Senate, where they held a majority. Hence, the party leadership, under the command of Eduardo Menem, called for a meeting of all Peronist senators to develop a strategy for defeating the legislation package.

The measure proved to be successful and the law was defeated. The Peronist Party and the unions then decided to develop a policy of systematic opposition to the administration's policies. While the Peronist Senate bloc originally supported many of the administration's policies, especially regarding the prosecution of the military leaders, they opposed most of the administration's subsequent initiatives. The unions also decided to increase their level of militancy. Indeed, the Alfonsin administration was paralyzed by thirteen general strikes between 1984 and 1989, thus exacerbating the country's economic decline.

As the economic situation continued its downward spiral, the Radicals increasingly lost their political power, and the dire economic situation reduced or removed many of the disposable resources the state used to control the political process (Canitrot and Sigal, 1992). The party's decline of power was strongly underscored by the 1987 elections. The Radicals lost their majority in the House of Deputies, along with the control of a number of provincial governments, and their numbers in the Senate also declined.[19] Faced with a dim chance of winning the 1989 election, the administration finally decided to address the nation's economic problems, but the situation had already begun spinning out of control. As a last-ditch ploy, the government announced the privatization of the national telephone company, Entel. The administration was in desperate need of a major economic victory if it hoped to have any chance of winning the 1989 presidential elections.

First Privatization Attempt

As discussed earlier, the Alfonsin administration decided in 1988 to revitalize the public sector. One of its economic initiatives was an intensive investment program in the telecommunications sector called Megatel, but the subsequent failure of the program forced the administration to take more drastic measures to revitalize the economy. The president's next action was to appoint Dr. Rodolfo Teragno to the Ministry of Public Works. Teragno, a Cambridge-educated economist, decided that Argentina had no option but to launch an extensive privatization program. This would allow the country to improve the performance of the public sector, reduce the fiscal deficit, and gather the necessary resources to service the foreign debt. The privatization program would begin with the sale of Entel, followed by the divestiture of the national airlines, Aerolineas Argentinas.

During the second quarter of 1988, the government began a series of secret negotiations with the major telephone companies until it found an interested buyer. Once the deal was privately negotiated, the Alfonsin administration then sent the whole package to the Congress for ratification on January 2, 1989. Surprisingly, public support for the sale of Entel was strong. A poll by Guillermo Bravo and Pessah showed that 59% of the population supported the sale of the telephone company (Hill and Abdala, 1993). The Peronists, however, were still determined to oppose the administration's initiatives, especially when the national elections were so close and they had a strong chance of winning the presidency. The Peronists, therefore, were not going to allow the Alfonsin administration to walk away with an easy victory.

Faced with probable rejection by the Peronist bloc, the administration decided to open the process to public debate. Teragno allowed the debates to be televised nationally, and there was talk of a national referendum on the privatization program. Although the administration's tactic produced a boost in public approval (approval of the privatization initiative soared to 85%), the clock was literally running out for the administration because the presidential campaign was now underway. The debate process forced the Peronists to clearly see the benefits of the privatization program, but they, nonetheless, decided to hold off support of the program until they controlled the presidency (Hill and Abdala, 1993). Under the leadership of Eduardo Menem, the Peronist bloc held a second Senate caucus in 1988, and decided to reject the privatization initiative.

The Second Privatization Attempt

The 1989 election saw the emergence of three leading political candidates. The first was Eduardo Angeloz of the Radical Party. He was the governor of Cordoba and, as a member of the incumbent party, should have held an advantage. Unfortunately, the poor state of the economy undermined much of his political support; hence, he was forced to distance himself from the Alfonsin administration's performance. Instead, he campaigned on promises of privatization and less state intervention.

The second candidate was Alvaro Alsogaray, the leader of the right-of-center, Union de Centro Democratico (UCeDe). Alsogaray was a former military officer and economy minister. He favored privatizing the state-owned companies, but he opposed the payment method that the Alfonsin government was going to use. He advocated using debt-equity swaps to reduce the country's debt burden. Indeed, privatization seemed to be openly supported during the campaign. A survey by Mora y Arahu Consultants showed that 70% of the people interviewed in Buenos Aires on the eve of the election supported privatization in general.

The third candidate was Carlos Menem from the Peronist party. Menem, governor of La Rioja, ran on the traditional Peronist platform of social justice and higher industrial productivity. Most of his macroeconomic policies, however, were vague and contradictory. There was some rhetoric on a debt moratorium and traditional statist policies, but he did not mention specifics (Acuña, 1993b.). Menem toured the country in a mobile home named the "Menemovil" and portrayed himself as a man of the people running against corruption.

Menem pledged that if elected, he would faithfully adhere to the Peronist creed, which postulated economic nationalism, strong state regulation of the economy, resumption of economic growth through direct government investment, and social justice in the form of income redistribution in favor of salary and wage earners. This gained him the support not only of the labor movement but also of the middle-class voters who had been frustrated by almost six years of unfulfilled economic promises. Voters in the provinces also supported Menem because his programs would allocate more government funds for rural areas. His campaign was a success, and on May 15, 1989, the Peronist Party swept control of the presidency and both houses of Congress. The economy, however, was plunged into virtual chaos as economic actors sensed a return to the old statist economic model that had been the root cause of the current malaise. Therefore, the inflation rate doubled, capital flight increased, external debt payments were suspended, and food riots erupted as the nation plunged into anarchy.[20]

The Alfonsin administration now faced the possibility of another military coup, but this time lacked the political resources to reverse it. The president did not think that his administration could survive until the December 10 inauguration date, and he offered to resign five months ahead of schedule. In return for accepting the presidency ahead of schedule and assuming a country in the midst of economic anarchy, President-elect Menem demanded the resignation of the entire Congress and a call for new elections. He argued that he needed extraordinary powers to put the country back in order. The Radicals resisted such a move, anticipating that it would probably lead to a wholesale defeat of the party. At the same time, President Alfonsin did not want to be responsible for taking control of the country away from the military, only to have it return to the military later on.

President-elect Menem then offered a compromise that allowed him to assume office five months early, with an agreement from the Radicals that during those five months they would support any legislation presented by the administration, including any conferring of special decree powers upon the national executive (Hill and Abdala, 1993). The Radicals grudgingly agreed, and the transfer of power took place on July 8, 1989. Hence, the compromise virtually eliminated any political opposition from the Radical Party and gave the president a wide range of power. In fact, Menem would encounter the greatest opposition from members of his own Peronist Party.

Given the dire situation, the Menem administration decided to alter its political strategy. In his first speech to the nation, the president announced that he was taking over a broken, devastated, and destitute nation (Iazzetta, 1993). Given the emergency situation, declared President Menem, he would have to make drastic changes in order to rescue the country, thus allowing him to break many of his campaign promises and forge ahead with a new set of economic plans that would restore stability.[21] Three weeks later, on July 20, 1989, he addressed the members of the stock exchange and declared that the concept of social justice was built on competition and the free market. The only role for the state could be that of organizing the market and ensuring the enforcement of rules (*La Nacion*, 1989a.). Furthermore, instead of forging ahead with the traditional Peronist allies, unions and small businesses, President Menem decided to create a new alliance with the center right and the large capital groups (Mora y Araujo, 1991).

One of President Menem's first acts was to appoint Miguel Roig as economy minister. Roig was a senior executive at Bunge y Born, a powerful food conglomerate that had traditionally opposed the government's statist and economic protectionist policies. It was starting to become clear that the new government would base its economic policy on privatization and market liberalization. Other government appointments also came from the industrial and business sectors (Acuña, 1993a).

The privatization program was launched in the first few weeks of the administration; however, privatization played a different role in the political strategy of the Menem administration. While privatization was an end in itself to the other national executives in the Southern Cone and the Alfonsin administration, the Menem administration used privatization as a means to garner the approval of key interest groups.[22]

Canitrot and Sigal (1992) have argued that the new administration realized that, given the gravity of the political and economic situation, it could not govern without the support of the business community and the far right. Therefore, as a concession to gain political support, President Menem offered to privatize the two companies that the previous administration had attempted to sell. In other words, even though the administration was in its honeymoon phase, it did not expend political capital to sell Entel.[23] This arrangement helps to explain why the president chose Maria Julia Alsogaray, the daughter of Alvaro Alsogaray, to spearhead the sale of Entel. Her condition for participating in the privatization process was that debt-equity swaps be used instead of a cash sale—a plank of her father's campaign platform during the 1989 campaign. Thus, opposition to the privatization program was virtually eliminated and the program sailed through the Congress. Nonetheless, President Menem must have realized that his window of opportunity was limited when he gave Alsogaray only 180 days to complete the whole process.

Interest Groups

The Argentine political system has always been especially interesting to students of political economy because power is spread out among well-organized groups and entrenched interests (Lewis, 1990). Open conflict between social agents acting on their own behalf is rare. Instead, conflicts are often carried out through actors that exert pressure on government decisions (Canitrot and Sigal, 1992). The analyses in the previous two sections have shown that this was indeed the case in the privatization of Entel. Groups that had a major stake in the future of the telephone company, such as labor unions and industrial suppliers, played pivotal roles in helping or hindering the sale of the company. Hence, they refused to help the government in completing the sale (Petrazzini, 1993). Other important groups, such as the military and landed bourgeoisie, also demanded a role in the process. Therefore, management of the interest group situation was a key component in securing the passage of the telephone privatization program,

The Alfonsin administration, however, was not very concerned with the role of interest groups in the Argentine political system. Despite a wide array of opposition to the program, it never attempted to accommodate any of the key interest groups or to cultivate them as allies. Petrazzini (1993) has argued that the Alfonsin administration's strategy in privatizing Entel was to insulate itself from domestic pressures and concentrate all power within the national executive. While this approach may have marginally increased Alfonsin's power, it isolated the frail administration from the resources of external groups.

The fact that the Alfonsin privatization program offered the telephone company to a foreign company and no participation to local industrial groups was considered a virtual insult to Argentine business leaders. The Argentina Chamber of Telecommunications went so far as to bring civil suit against Teragno for attempting to establish a private monopoly in violation of Argentine antitrust laws (*La Nacion*, July 26, 1989b).

Alfonsin's policies had already alienated most of the country's major political and economic groups. The military was put though a series of humiliating trials, the landed bourgeoisie continued to suffer from the government's protectionist economic policies, and the administration attempted to restructure the unions through a new labor legislation package.[24] Therefore, President Alfonsin could count on very little political support to ratify the privatization program. Furthermore, the poor economic situation removed many of the resources that the administration could have used to elicit cooperation from smaller social groups.

President Menem, however, had a different approach. His strategy was to build coalitions and provide side payments to ensure cooperation. One of the first groups he tried to mollify was the military. President Menem announced that he wanted to leave Argentina's history of military rule and the resulting show trials behind, and push on with rebuilding the economy. Soon after his inauguration, the president issued 200 pardons to military officers and personnel who had been convicted in the human rights trials. He also took steps to increase the level of professionalism in the military by propping up the General Staff (Acuña, 1993a). And finally, he announced the privatization of the national defense industries (DGFM), thus allowing the military to benefit from the new economic policies (Manzetti, 1993). With DGFM assets valued at $5.6 billion and with annual sales of $1.2 billion, the military leadership was assured of collecting some of the spoils from the privatization initiative. The administration also promised the military that some of the proceeds would be used to purchase military equipment and pay for increases in officers' salaries.[25]

President Menem gained the approval of the landed bourgeoisie by naming an executive from Bunge y Born as economy minister.[26] He also redesigned the privatization program to allow the national industrial groups to participate in the ownership of the companies. President Menem did not need to court the unions, however, since they, along with the associations of small business leaders, formed the backbone of the Peronist Party (Gaudio, Thompson, and Garcia, 1993). His loyalty to the unions was suspect even from the time of the campaign. Although his campaign rhetoric had centered on social justice, his language promised aid to the *poor*, and was not the traditional Peronist promises of aid to workers.[27] It is important to note, however, that President Menem did make important concessions to labor. His selection of CGT leader Jorge Triaca as labor minister and letting union bosses retain control of the welfare and social funds strengthened the alliance between the administration and the unions.

In regard to the telephone worker's union (FOETRA) the Menem administration made several key concessions. In addition to offering 10% of the new company shares, he named the union leader, Julio Guillan, as secretary of communications. This was a temporary concession to the unions, since the office of the secretary of communications would disappear after the privatization was complete, replaced by a new regulatory organization called CNT (Herrera, 1992). Factions in the union, however, refused to comply with the government's program and in August 1990 organized a national strike that disconnected Argentine telephones from the world (Petrazzini, 1993). As expected from the Schattschneider framework, the weaker side tried to expand the scope of the conflict. However, President Menem immediately called in the

Army to occupy the central offices and operate the lines. He then fired 400 workers who refused to return to work.

But President Menem's concerns with reducing the "Argentine cost" of doing business resulted in a severe blow to labor. Ever since 1987, Argentine industrial output had been declining, and he wanted to reverse the trend (Damill and Frenkel, 1990). In Argentina's case, the best way to increase the level of productivity was to reduce employment levels and cut wages (Durchslag, Puri, and Rao, 1994). However, this would require breaking the power of the unions, suppressing wage indexation, and increasing the flexibility of labor.

The only remaining opposition to the privatization program came from elements within Menem's own party who opposed the dismantling of the state-enterprise system. The Peronist Party was still a collection of extreme right and left ideologies that coexisted in a party based on labor and the poor (Waisman, 1990). Few elements in the party espoused neoliberal economic reforms. In order to overcome opposition from traditional elements of the Peronist Party, the president transferred much of the power to his brother, Eduardo Menem, president of the Senate and head of the Peronist bloc. Thus, by giving the Congress the perception of having a greater voice in the design of the economic programs, he was able to ensure its support.

Unable to provide side payments to all parties, President Menem made a concerted effort to control smaller groups and individuals who opposed the privatization program (Manzetti, 1993). For example, Inspector General Alberto Gonzalez Arzac, who raised strong criticisms of the program, was forced to quit. Federal Prosecutor Oscar Garzon Funes, who also opposed the privatization program, was barred by the Supreme Court from investigating a charge by Congressman Moises Fontela of governmental wrong doing in the privatization program. All-in-all, Menem's strategy of managing key interest groups allowed him to push through a series of necessary and painful economic reforms reestablishing stability in Argentina.

Institutional Constraints

While the selective use of side payments was instrumental in controlling the major Argentine interest groups, the Menem administration also implemented some important institutional changes to concentrate the national executive's power and ensure the implementation of his economic reforms and privatization programs (Acuña, 1993b). One such move was the reorganization of the Supreme Court. In 1990, President Menem increased the number of Supreme Court justices from seven to fifteen (Hill and Abdala, 1993). Since the Peronists had a majority in the Senate, he was able to appoint new justices who would be sympathetic to his policies, thus ensuring support for his programs.

Hill and Abdala (1993) have argued that the structure of Argentine electoral rules hindered the cohesion of the political parties. Since Argentine deputies and senators represent provinces, they have narrowly defined points of views that often do not coincide with the national party's objectives. This has allowed the proliferation of provincial parties at the expense of the national parties. Furthermore, the staggering of the elections, so that half of the deputies and one-third of the senators are elected at the same time as the president, has reduced the incentive to unify the federal and provincial party organizations. The result has been the tendency to produce divided and partisan Congresses, especially in the situation of minority governments—as was the case during the first attempt to privatize Entel. It took a major event, the Radical attempt to sever the union and party linkages, to mobilize the Peronist Party. The Peronists later pushed through their policies because of the abdication agreement the Radicals made with President Menem.

Another of the institutional factors that boosted Menem's ability to privatize Entel was the relationship between the Peronist Party and the unions. Although Frieden (1991) has argued that the cooperation between labor and government depends on the perceived gains or losses of the interested parties, it does not explain why the Argentine labor unions cooperated so closely with the government's privatization and economic policies—many of which were designed to curtail the power of the unions. Ironically, it was the same linkages between the Peronist Party and the union leadership that the Alfonsin administration tried unsuccessfully to sever that were binding the union leadership to Menem's policies. Since the Peronist Party could manipulate the union structure, labor leaders were forced to acquiesce to government policies. Kelsey and Levitsky (1994) described this phenomenon as *"captivating alliances"* and used it to explain why the unions in Argentina and Mexico supported economic reform policies that ultimately reduced the power of the unions and employment levels (Murillo, 1994).

The political factors offer a great deal of insight into the process of privatization. The use of the theoretical framework assembled from the literature on development and U.S. politics provides an excellent mechanism to examine the relative power of the principal groups and institutions.

The case material suggests that of the three factors that help determine the power of the national executive—congressional support, time in office, and economic situation—the first two were the most important. While President Lacalle of Uruguay and Alfonsin enjoyed high levels of popularity early part in their administrations, they used their honeymoon periods to implement other types of reforms, leaving privatization policies to later. However, their lack of congressional support left them unable to push through the subsequent policy changes. Unfortunately, the honeymoon period of President Collor of Brazil was virtually nonexistent due to his confrontational approach and his lack of political support in the Congress. The situation in Chile was different because the privatization occurred in a nondemocratic setting. In other words, there was no political opposition. President Menem, however, was able to implement the privatization policies because he launched the initiative early in his administration and had strong support in both houses of Congress.

The cases also show how the principal actors reacted to stimuli according to expectations. As suggested by Schattschneider (1960), the weaker parties usually sought an expansion of the conflict in order to shift or reverse the balance of power. Furthermore, institutions played the greatest role in situations where there was a relative equal balance of power.

The material also underscores the importance of the transition to democracy on the overall power of the executive. As suggested by the literature on presidentialism, the initial arrangements made during the transition from authoritarian rule established the capacity of the national executive to implement policy changes. Furthermore, the military clearly was a destabilizing force in all of the cases.[28] With the exception of Chile, where the military dominated politics, it often sapped the administration's scarce resources. President Alfonsin was limited in his range of policy options due to the series of military uprisings that plagued his administration. President Menem was able to neutralize the military by providing important concessions, including pardoning convicted officers and granting the General Staff the right to freely use the proceeds from the sale of military industries. In Uruguay, as the country moved forward with its economic reforms, the military demanded immediate settlement of outstanding pay issues. The Brazilian military wanted consultation on all policy issues and opposed the sale of the state-owned enterprises.

The sense of economic emergency was not as significant as the literature suggested. Although Presidents Collor and Alfonsin both faced dire economic situations, they were not able to sell their telephone companies. The sense of economic emergency helped President Menem assume office ahead of schedule, but it did not gain him more power. Indeed, it was fear of the impending military coup that enhanced his initial power to implement policy.

As suggested by the theoretical framework, institutions played the biggest role in cases where there was a relative stability in the balance of power. The Brazilian case showed that the absence of either a dominant president, legislature, or interest groups allowed institutional rules, such as constitutional restrictions on the privatization of strategic companies, to prevent the sale of Telebras. This is not so surprising, given the short history of Latin American democracy. Institutions probably have not had time to develop and mature. Hence, their capacity to shape events is limited, especially when confronted by strong political actors; however, when the political forces are weak, the institutions may become more significant.

All in all, the section on the political factors was very instrumental in presenting and analyzing the noneconomic factors that affect the process of privatization. The use of political, as well as microeconomic and macroeconomic variables allows for a better understanding of the dynamic forces facing developing countries, particularly when they seek to implement major policy changes. This analysis emphasizes that the use of political variables is a central component in establishing a better understanding of the development process.

CONCLUSION

The Argentine case provides a slightly different view on the role of macroeconomic factors in the privatization process. It is evident that the country suffered from serious macroeconomic crises and that the privatization option was a natural policy choice to help solve the problem. The deficit generated by the state-owned companies virtually paralyzed the nation; and the lack of access to foreign capital, due to the outstanding debt obligations, dimmed any prospects for growth. However, there were few differences between the magnitudes of the economic crises surrounding the two Argentine privatization attempts. Nonetheless, the outcomes were different. During both attempts the country experienced huge public-sector deficits, hyperinflation, and unmanageable foreign debts. This is very different from the Uruguayan case, where there also were two outcomes but the macroeconomic situation evolved between the election of President Lacalle and the ANTEL plebiscite. Therefore, the macroeconomic factors do not provide a complete picture of the pressures affecting the privatization decision.

Entel was clearly a poorly managed and inefficient firm. Almost fifty years of state ownership resulted in a highly politicized unit where the emphasis was on rent seeking and political favors. Despite the poor financial, material, and managerial condition of the company, the government of President Raul Alfonsin was unable to sell Entel. The Peronist government of Carlos Menem opposed the sale in 1988 but then was able to implement the process in 1990. Hence, the privatization of Entel had to do less with its microeconomic performance than with the political situation, thus reinforcing the findings of the earlier case studies.

The microeconomic analyses of the four cases provided several important insights. The first is that performance is an important factor in understanding the pressure to privatize. Firms that are well run do not enjoy the same level of support for divestiture as do firms that are poorly managed. As suggested at the beginning of the chapter, firm performance serves as a partial proxy for consumer sentiment. Nonetheless, it is not a perfect proxy. It served well for ANTEL in Uruguay. One of the arguments used against the privatization was that Uruguay had one of the best telephone systems in the world; therefore, what would be the gains of divestiture? The second insight was that decisions made regarding technology and equipment manufacturing placed countries on certain paths of development. Once the decision was made to enter the path, the country was committed to a narrow band of choices delimited by its own resources. By locking themselves into technological designs or manufacturing obligations, the countries also created opportunity spaces for interest groups to develop and exert high levels of control while collecting high rents. Countries, such as Argentina and Brazil, that developed domestic capacities for manufacturing telecommunications equipment also created strong political interest groups that not only depended on the continuation of the state telephone company but also shaped the direction of activity in the company. In the case of Argentina, the domestic equipment manufacturers were not a party to the first privatization plan and were opposed to the initiative, but they fully endorsed the second attempt when they were allowed to become a party to the divestiture.

It is clear that microeconomic performance provides important insights into the process of privatization; however, it does not provide sufficient insight to explain variations in the phenomenon. Surprisingly, the level of firm performance failed to correlate with the privatization outcomes. While much of the economics literature suggested that companies with low levels of performance would be the more likely candidates for privatization, the impact was random. Some relatively inefficient companies, such as Telebras, were not privatized, while more efficient operations, such as CTC, were sold. The case studies reveal that there are other forces driving the privatization process. They also show that privatization clearly engages political questions. The divestiture of these companies had much to do with the power of the national executive and the interest groups that were in favor of, or in opposition to the privatization program.

The analysis of the macroeconomic factors makes an interesting contribution to the analysis of privatization. The data suggested that country-level factors offer an important insight into the forces driving the decision to privatize. Most of the cases revealed situations where inefficient state-owned companies placed excessive burdens on thin government resources. Indeed, Devlin (1992) found that by incorporating net transfers between the government and SOEs, the fiscal situation often improved. Therefore, governments considered privatization as an opportunity to solve the economic crisis and to open access to additional levels of investment.

The operationalization of the comparative macroeconomic data reveals that the only consistent macroeconomic factor the countries shared was high fiscal deficits. Table 23 contains five general categories: fiscal balance, inflation, GDP growth rate, relative debt level, and debt servicing levels By using a simple categorization of low, moderate, or high, the table reveals that GDP growth and the debt situation had little impact on the privatization process or outcomes.

Table 23
Comparison of Influence of Macroeconomic Factors on Privatization Outcomes

	Fiscal Balance	Inflation	GDP Growth	Debt Levels	Debt Service	Outcomes
Argentina	Very high fiscal deficit	Hyper-inflation	Negative	High	High	Rejected/ accepted
Brazil	High deficit	Hyper-inflation	Positive	Low	Moderate	Postponed
Chile	Moderate deficit	Moderate	Positive	High	Moderate	Accepted
Uruguay	Surplus	Moderate	Positive	Moderate	Moderate	Rejected

Hence, the analysis of the case material suggests that macroeconomic factors help to explain the decision to consider the privatization as an economic policy alternative, but they provide no insight on the timing of implementation. Fiscal deficits are clearly a necessary condition for a privatization initiative to be launched, but they are not a sufficient condition for initiation or even implementation.[29] Furthermore, GDP performance, inflation, and foreign debt were only marginally important in the privatization decision. Nonetheless, the debt-equity swaps seemed to play an important role in luring in foreign investors. By offering holders of sovereign debt an opportunity to trade their highly discounted debt instruments for shares in privatized companies, countries created an opportunity to attract foreign investors while reducing their debt obligations. Indeed, this was the case in Argentina and Chile. Once investors have been attracted, then other investors followed, thus increasing the level of foreign investment and helping to spur economic development. Last, pressures from the multilateral lending agencies were inconclusive. The agencies placed pressure on countries to divest SOEs, but it was not binding. They created teams to provide advice and offered resources to help structure privatizations. Many of the countries eventually used the programs, but the mere presence of the multilateral pressure did not give any indication of when it would be done. This seemed to be more of a political consideration.

From the perspective of some social scientists, the macroeconomic factors are the driving force behind privatization and can indicate whether a privatization will occur. For many other social scientists, timing is an important factor. It is not enough to say that eventually Argentina would privatize its telephone company: when is an important consideration. It has much to do with the allocation of capital, the timing of reforms to coincide with international conditions, and social impact. It also provides some insight into the political conditions that are needed to start a major structural reform program.

The findings in these case studies coincide with some other studies on privatization. Nankani (1990) found that many countries with large macroeconomic problems and vast numbers of SOEs often failed to privatize anything.[30] Indeed, Kahler (1989, 1992) found that the influence of the IMF and

World Bank on the sustained direction of economic policy was limited to a few cases; governments and interest groups resisted the intrusion of external agencies, and attempted to slow or halt policy changes through the political process. Sachs (1989) came to a similar conclusion. Therefore, the factors affecting privatization policies remain illusive. More explanatory power should be found in the analysis of the political hypothesis, especially since political explanations may be able to provide more insights when economic explanations are clearly insufficient.

Last of all, the Argentine cases are very good examples of the Schattschneider theoretical framework. Presidents Alfonsin and Menem initially enjoyed great political power when they assumed the presidency. Alfonsin's honeymoon period was based on the euphoria over Argentina's return to democratic rule. He used it to consolidate the newly established democracy by limiting the power of the military and attempting to reduce the power of the Peronist Party. By the time he sought to sell the telephone company, however, the honeymoon period was long past and the marriage had begun to sour. Faced with diminishing power, the embattled administration tried to isolate itself from domestic interest groups. When the situation looked worse, it decided to open the debate to the public in order to shift the balance of power in its favor; despite its best efforts, the administration increasingly lost control of the process. With the election campaign in full swing, the privatization initiative was lost in the rush of events and subsided into the background.

In contrast, President Menem's "honeymoon" period was based on a sense of urgency and crisis. Menem argued that he needed ample powers to restore order to the situation and rescue the country. The president, however, must have realized his limited time frame when he ordered the privatization of Entel to be completed in under 180 days. Hence, he was able to implement the privatization of Entel during the time period when his power was high and he was able to control the privatization process.

Therefore, the two Argentine cases provide important insights to the privatization case studies. The two Argentine cases confirm that the power of the national executive is the pivotal factor in the shaping and managing the privatization process. The resources that the Argentine national executives had at their disposal were very important in providing the side-payments needed to secure cooperation from key interest groups. As Schattschneider (1960) argued, failure to have the necessary resources to control the process only led to an expansion of the debate by the weaker party. This altered the balance of power, and it also led to a loss of control. Given the relative imbalance of power in the two situations, it is not surprising that the institutional factors were not very significant. While they helped cement labor's cooperation with the Peronist Party, these factors did not alter the direction of the privatization process.

NOTES

1. The Peronists launched a publicity campaign declaring that the sale would grant the British crown control of Argentine telecommunications. Peronist Senator Luis Rubeo based his allegations on a recent strategic agreement between the Spanish and British telephone companies. The ploy was an attempt to incite anti-British feelings in Argentina.

2. Gerchunoff (1993) notes that the rate hike increased Entel's revenue stream by 90% in real terms, thus boosting its attractiveness.

3. The purchase of the Argentine telephone company was a central part of the demarcation arrangement between AT&T and ITT struck by J.P. Morgan. In return for unrestricted access to the international market, ITT agreed not to enter the US market, thus providing AT&T with an uncontested monopoly in the United States. With the assistance of J.P. Morgan capital, ITT built up an international telecommunications empire that spanned the globe. It included the Spanish telephone company, Telefonica, and the telephone companies of Chile and Argentina. (Chernow, 1990).

4. ITT would retain a presence in Argentina until the early 1980s, operating the equipment manufacturer Equitel (Herrera, 1989). The company management found that equipment manufacturing provided higher rates of return than telephone operations.

5. Megatel was an expansion plan that would add an additional 1 million new lines.

6. In 1988, the Public Works Ministry estimated that Entel spent an extra $2 billion on goods and services because it was forced to purchase mostly Argentine produced equipment.

7. In June 1993, as part of an anticorruption sweep, the Italian ambassador to Argentina was convicted by an Italian court of receiving kickbacks on contracts given to Entel.

8. The two factions had been broken apart during the military repression, called *el proceso*. The union organizations had continued to exist underground. CGT-Azopardo eventually came to cooperate with the military government, while CGT-RA was much more confrontational. After the return to democracy, the two groups hesitated to merge until the attempt by the Alfonsin government to reform organized labor (Blake, 1992).

9. As was the case in the other Latin American economies, the statist and ISI systems were largely built on the backs of strong agricultural exports. These statist policies advocated a closed economy and protectionist policies, while agriculture producers supported an open economy, low tariffs, and a cheap currency. The landed bourgeois had been strong advocates of privatization since the 1940s. Argentina's major institutional groups, Sociedad Rural, was strongly opposed to President Alfonsin's programs. Indeed, at the end of his administration in 1988, its members loudly booed president at the opening ceremony of the organization's annual fair.

10. IMF stabilization plans are unpopular due to the austerity of the measures. Their programs, usually very successful in reinstating price stability, often include the balancing of the fiscal accounts and the liberalization of the economy and exchange rate.

11. Another inherent flaw of heterodox stabilization programs is their tendency to induce erratic patterns of economic growth. As Table 15 illustrates, this was clearly the case in Argentina. The different programs introduced by the Alfonsin ad-

ministration put the country onto a roller-coaster ride of GDP ups and downs. This type of economic pattern is more damaging than a consistent pattern of growth. It does not allow economic actors to plan any type of outlook for the future.

12. The provinces amassed a great deal of political and economic power during the military regimes. Faced with limited resources and huge territorial responsibilities, the military leadership gave them high levels of independence and allowed them to share federal revenues in the form of subsidies and guarantees. In return, the provinces pledged their acquiescence to the military rulers. Thus, the military forces could concentrate most of their resources on controlling the major urban centers, such as Buenos Aires (Canitrot and Sigal, 1992).

13. The first foreign loan was issued in London in 1824. It was by Baring Brothers, for £1 million, for the construction of fortifications on the cattle frontier. Half of the loan went for fees and commissions. The first Argentine default on a foreign loan occurred three years later. In 1827, Brazil's attempt to invade Montevideo resulted in a Brazilian blockade which then reduced port revenues and forced Argentina to default on the Baring loan. This default precipitated a major crisis in the London financial markets. The next debt crisis occurred after the Franco-Prussian War in 1871. France's defeat and subsequent economic disarray resulted in a decline British exports and a payments deficit. Britain responded by raising its discount rate, thus leading to a decline in clothing manufacturing and the collapse of demand for Argentine hides and wool.

14. Although not a multilateral lending agency, the Spanish government played a major role in the privatization of Entel. Due to Spain's strong support of the Alfonsin government during the transition to democracy, some Argentine officials felt that it should be granted with preferential treatment in the sale of the telephone company.

15. The Malvinas defeat produced profound cleavages within the armed forces. First, there was a breakdown in interforce relations during the latter stages of the dictatorship. The Navy and the Air Force withdrew from the military junta and refused to participate in the election of General Reynaldo Bignone as president. Second, a horizontal cleavage developed, separating generals who held positions of responsibility for the Army's policies and actions from subordinates who had been on the front lines.

16. Indeed, Przerworski (1986) argued that transitions from authoritarian rule tend to create a difficult collective action problem whereby leaders of groups, such as unions, will tend to withhold their cooperation as long as a viable alternative exists.

17. The Peronists held twenty-one seats, and the Radicals held eighteen. The rest were held by the provincial parties.

18. Unfortunately, this was a poor assumption. The international financial community demanded immediate settlement of the country's debts and restricted further capital inflows until it did so, thus precipitating Argentina's economic decline and the Alfonsin administration's downfall.

19. The 1987 elections reduced the number of Radical Senate seats from eighteen to fourteen and increased the number of Peronist Senators from twenty-one to twenty-four. At the same time, the Radicals lost sixteen seats in the House of Deputies for a total of 113, while the Peronists increased their presence from 101 to 103 seats.

Thus, when taking into account the other minority and provincial parties, the Radicals no longer held a majority in the House of Deputies.

20. Even television commentators were pleading for a "return to reality" as images of stark poverty, violence, and looting were transmitted to Argentine homes (Canitrot and Sigal, 1992).

21. When pressed for his reasons for abandoning his original economic policies, Menem retorted that he had received a political mandate from the Argentine people, but not an economic one (Packenham, 1994).

22. Furthermore, the way that the privatization sale was structured removed the remaining opposition by telecommunication equipment manufacturers. The newly formed companies would have to purchase at least 25% of their equipment and supplies from local vendors. Last of all, the Argentine company assumed all of Entel's debts, including those owed to equipment manufacturing firms, thus ensuring their settlement.

23. It was not until after the sale of Entel that the administration realized the immense success of the privatization program. It was then that President Menem accepted full credit for the program and went on to expand the process to the rest of the Argentine SOEs.

24. The open disregard of the agricultural sector for the Alfonsin government was evidenced by the hostile reception the president received at the 102nd annual exposition of the Sociedad Rural (Anales de la Sociedad Rural, 1988).

25. Despite the concessions made to the military, on December 3, 1990, a dissident group of officers, known as the Carapintadas, staged an uprising. It was brutally subverted by the General Staff, and the officers were severely punished by the military courts. This put an end to the military confrontations for the rest of the administration

26. The impact of the incorporation of agricultural interests into the new government was evident when President Menem received a standing ovation at the 1989 Sociedad Rural exposition. At the opening ceremonies, he promised to reduce all export tariffs from 20% to 0% in two months, reform the tariff system, and reintroduce financing for export products (La Nacion, 1989c).

27. Canitrot and Sigal (1992) argue that part of Menem's move away from worker groups was attributed to the decline of organized labor in Argentina. The deindustrialization of the country in the 1970s and 1980s and the growth of the service sector had reduced the power of traditional labor unions.

28. This observation is in agreement with Kimenyi and Mbaku's (1993) paper, which argued that of all the rent-seeking groups competing in society, the military were the most destabilizing.

29. This is consistent with an observation by Haggard and Kaufman (1992) that the perception of fiscal crisis is a necessary, but not a sufficient condition for the divestiture of public enterprises.

30. Nankani gives the example of Sri Lanka. In 1977, it announced a huge program of reducing its public sector, but it divested only 11 out of 180 SOEs.

6

CONCLUSION:
GENERALIZING THE ARGUMENT

The case studies presented in the previous four chapters examined the different forces that shaped the privatization process in the Southern Cone of Latin America. Each case examined the individual microeconomic, macroeconomic, and political factors. The cases showed that microeconomic factors were not very significant in determining privatization outcomes; macroeconomic factors were found to be more important. Indeed, the case materials showed that fiscal deficits played an important role in motivating the countries to consider privatization policies. The political factors, nonetheless, proved to contain the most powerful explanatory power. The case study materials showed that the power of the national executive, as measured by the percentage of the legislative body that held a similar political affiliation, indicated the government's ability to implement privatization policies. While the case studies provided an important insight into the process of structural adjustment in a particular region of Latin America, they did not indicate their efficacy in the rest of the world. Therefore, in order to generalize the findings of the four case studies, I have expanded the scope of analysis to include the other regions of the developed and developing world.

At the end of the first chapter, three general questions were posed to help guide the analytical process. The questions asked about the ability of microeconomic, macroeconomic, and political factors to explain privatization outcomes. Now that I am generalizing the findings of the case studies, I will transform the questions into three general hypotheses.

H1:   Poor microeconomic performance of state-owned telephone companies in-
           creases the likelihood that countries will approve the privatization programs.

H2:   Poor macroeconomic conditions should motivate countries to approve the pri-
           vatization of state-owned companies.

H3:   The approval of privatization programs is contingent on the political strength
           of the national executive.

These three hypotheses, however, are very general propositions, and
they do not facilitate data testing. Therefore, I have split each hypothesis into
two smaller propositions to allow examination of the relationships between the
different factors and outcomes—in other words, the independent and dependent
variables.

H1: Microeconomic Hypotheses

H1.A: Governments will tend to approve the sale of state-owned telephone companies
that have lower levels of efficiency, as measured by number of telephone lines per
worker.

H1.B: Governments will have a tendency to approve the sale of state-owned telephone
companies that have had lower levels of investment and expansion, as measured by the
number of telephone lines per inhabitant.

H2: Macroeconomic Hypotheses

H2.A: Governments with low GDP growth will be apt to approve the sale of state-
owned enterprises.

H2.B: Governments with high fiscal deficits will tend to approve the sale of state-owned
enterprises.

H3: Political Hypotheses

H3.A: Chief executives with congressional majorities will tend to receive approval for
the sale of state-owned enterprises.

H3.B: Chief executives will tend to get approval for the privatization of state-owned
enterprises during the early part of their administrations.

The benefit of this exercise was to employ a battery of statistical tests
to analyze the efficacy of the three general hypotheses and create a more gen-
eralized set of conclusions. Therefore, the next step in the testing process required the construction of a small database using the major variables identified
in the case studies and hypotheses. All of the variables were then normalized
according to GDP or population, so as to aid the comparative analyses. The
two microeconomic variables were *telephone lines per worker* and *telephone*

lines per 100 inhabitants. The data were obtained from the International Telephone Union's 1995 database on global communications.

GDP growth rate and the *fiscal deficit as a percentage of GDP* were the two macroeconomic variables selected. The country statistics were obtained from the 1995 International Financial Statistics database that is prepared each month by the International Monetary Fund. The third set of variables was the political factors—the presence of a *majority* in the legislature and the amount of *time in office.* These data were obtained from various sources, including *The Political Handbook of the World. Majority* was coded 0 if the national executive had less than 50% of the legislature with the same party affiliation; otherwise it was coded 1. The *time in office* was calculated as the time between inauguration and the approval of the privatization legislation. Table 24 presents the global database of all attempted privatizations of telecommunication companies between 1981 and 1995.

Table 24
Global Comparative Statistics of Attempted Privatizations, 1981–1995

Country and Company Name	Micro Variable		Macro Variable		Political Variable		
	Lines per Worker	Lines Per 100 People	GDP	Fiscal Balance	Majority in Congress	Time in Office	Out-come
United Kingdom (BT)	74	33	-1.3	-2.6	1	884	Accept
Japan (NTT)	141	37	4.3	-2.1	1	487	Accept
Chile (CTC/ENTEL)	72	5	2.4	-6.9	1	4,505	Accept
Jamaica (JTC)	34	3	1.6	-1.3	1	2,372	Accept
Argentina I (ENTEL)	81	9	2.6	-3.6	0	1,644	Reject
Mexico (TELMEX)	96	4	6.5	-2.4	1	274	Accept
Venezuela (CANTV)	75	8	-8.6	-1.7	0	31	Accept
Thailand (TOT/CAT)	61	2	13.3	-0.9	0	3,348	Reject
Argentina II (ENTEL)	73	11	-6.2	-2.6	1	61	Accept
New Zealand (NZ TELECOM)	103	45	3	-3.9	1	274	Accept
South Africa (SAPT)	34	8	2.3	-2.7	0	273	Reject
Malaysia (JTM)	56	9	9.7	-3	1	31	Accept
Brazil (TELEBRAS)	49	6	0.9	-22.7	0	577	Reject
Colombia (TELECOM)	200	8	2.3	-0.3	1	701	Reject
Uruguay (ANTEL)	66	14	2.9	-0.6	0	1,157	Reject
Greece (OTE)	152	38	0	-12.5	0	1,310	Reject
Singapore (ST)	193	47	5.8	0	1	1,126	Accept
Peru (ENTEL)	86	3	4.2	-1.7	1	1,359	Accept
Pakistan (PTC)	24	1	3.1	0	0	396	Accept
Hungary (MATAZ)	93	17	3.0	-4.2	1	2,082	Accept
India (VSNL)	24	1	6.4	-6.7	0	1,208	Reject
Bolivia (ENTEL)	130	3	5.0	-2.6	0	2,369	Accept
Czech (SPT)	86	21	4.0	0	1	1,857	Accept

STATISTICAL ANALYSIS

In order to examine the wide range of numerical information and analyze the six hypotheses, we put the data through a series of statistical tests. The first test employed summary statistics. This tabular analysis allowed the use of summary information, including averages, standard deviations, maxima, and minima. The second set of tests were univariate analyses that allowed the testing of each of the six hypotheses. There was an attempt to use Logit as a multivariate test to examine the interrelation between the independent and dependent variable; however, due to the low number of observations and the strong collinear relationship between the political variables and the outcomes, the *t* statistics were not significant.

SUMMARY STATISTICS

The calculation of the summary statistics required the segmentation of the database into two groups, privatization cases that were rejected and those that were accepted. Tables 25 and 26 present the two sets of summary statistics for the privatizations. Contrary to the expectations set by the microeconomic literature, company performance, as measured by the *number of telephone lines per worker*, did not vary inversely to privatization outcomes. In other words, countries that had companies with poorer levels of efficiency tended not to privatize their telephone companies. The results for the second set of microeconomic statistics, the *penetration rate* or *number of telephone lines per 100 inhabitants*, also contradicted the literature. The academic literature on microeconomic factors argued that operational and managerial inefficiencies were propelling SOEs toward change, and the vehicle for this change was privatization. The summary data material, however, showed that, on average, the privatization of poorly performing companies around the world was rejected. These findings were consistent with those in the four Southern Cone cases. Indeed, the case material found that company performance had very little to do with privatization outcomes. In fact, poor company performance usually indicated the presence of strong interest groups that dominated the telephone company, thus extracting huge rents and leading to poor operating results.

Table 25
Summary Statistics of Rejected Privatizations, N= 8

	Workers	Penetration	Growth	Deficit	Congress	Time
Average	83.38	10.75	3.84	-6.25	0.13	1277.25
Standard Deviation	200.00	38.00	13.30	-0.30	1.00	3348.00
Maximum	24.00	1.00	0.00	-22.70	0.00	273.00
Minimum	61.25	11.74	4.25	0.00	0.35	946.71

Table 26
Summary Statistics of Accepted Privatizations, N=15

	Workers	Penetration	Growth	Deficit	Congress	Time
Average	89.07	16.49	2.43	-2.33	0.80	1207.20
Standard Deviation	193.00	47.30	9.70	0.00	1.00	4505.00
Maximum	24.00	1.00	-8.60	-6.90	0.00	31.00
Minimum	42.08	16.27	4.69	0.00	0.41	1250.79

While the macroeconomic statistics did not completely contradict the corresponding literature, as was the case with the microeconomic output, the results were mixed. The summary results showed that, in concert with macro-economic expectations, countries with high *GDP growth rates* tended to reject privatization initiatives, while those with lower *GDP growth* rates accepted them. These findings mirrored the results in the case studies. However, the summary information also showed that countries with high *fiscal deficits* tended to reject privatization policies. These findings are interesting because *fiscal deficits* were one of the most important motivating factors in the Southern Cone cases.

Yet, a closer look at the data reveals an interesting insight. The average *fiscal deficit* for all of the cases was 3.7%, while the best fiscal balance was 0–this was recorded in only two cases. Hence, almost all of the countries seeking privatization of their telephone companies were in fiscal distress. This observation confirms Haggard and Kaufman's (1992) finding that the perception of a fiscal crisis is a necessary, but not a sufficient, condition for the divestiture of public enterprises. The results of the summary statistics may suggest that extreme fiscal crises could be an indication of other more telling problems, such as a weak government or entrenched interest groups, that prevented the sale of the state companies.

Although the microeconomic factors turned out to be very disappointing, and the macroeconomic results were mixed, the political factors contained the most explanatory power. In 80% of the cases where privatization was accepted, the president had a *majority* in the legislature, whereas a *majority* was available in only 13% of the rejected cases. The amount of *time in office* of the national executive also proved to be in line with the literature, but the data suggested that it was not very significant.

UNIVARIATE ANALYSIS

While the summary statistics shed light on the aggregate figures, a univariate analysis is a more sophisticated approach to statistically testing diverse groups of data. This format allows the testing of individual hypotheses, thus providing an indication of how the global data fit the expectations generated by the literature and the four case studies. This particular analysis consisted of a *t*-test analysis on the accepted privatizations (coded AP) and rejected privatizations (RP). Table 27 presents the differences in the means for the six relevant variables across the two categories. The last column indicates the differences in means matched the hypothesized sign.

Table 27
Differences in Means of Microeconomic, Macroeconomic, and Political Variables

Hypothesis/ Variable	Rejected Privatization (RP)	Accepted Privatization (AP)	Difference (RP-NP)	Hypothesis	Result
H1: Microeconomic Variables					
H1.A: Lines per Workers	83.37	89.07	-5.70	RP>AP	Rejected
H1.B: Penetration Rate	10.75	16.49	-5.74	RP> AP	Rejected
H2: Macroeconomic Variables					
H2.A: GDP Growth	3.84	2.43	1.41	RP>AP	Accepted
H2.B: Fiscal Deficit	-6.25	-2.33	-3.92	RP>AP	Rejected
H3: Political Variables					
H3.A: Congressional Majority	0.12	0.80	-0.68	AP>RP	Accepted
H3.B: Time in Office	1,277.25	1,207.20	70.05	RP>AP	Accepted

(Note: Significance based on one-tailed *t*-test using pooled variance, $p < 0.05$)

Not surprisingly, the results in Table 27 were exactly in line with the findings produced by the summary statistics. The univariate analysis rejected both of the microeconomic hypotheses. In the twenty-three privatization attempts recorded between 1981 and 1995, countries with inefficient telephone operations were less likely to complete the privatization process. The macroeconomic results also mirrored the mixed results obtained in the summary statistics. Countries with lower GDP growth were more likely to privatize, while those with severe fiscal deficits were less likely to divest their state assets. Last of all, the univariate analysis accepted both political hypotheses. Countries where the national executive had a majority in the Congress were much more successful in selling their state-owned telephone companies. The results also showed that countries where the national executive had less than 12 months in office were also more likely to privatize. Yet, the margin between the two groups was not very important. The difference between the two groups was only seventy days, or a little over two months—hardly a honeymoon period.

CONCLUSIONS

Microeconomic Factors

Although the information in the global database suggests that company factors were not significant for understanding the process of privatization, the case material provided a different conclusion. The cases showed that the historical and technological development of each telephone company was a crucial element in identifying the political and economic forces surrounding the national telecommunications sector. This contextual information provided the key to recognizing the core interest groups, public sentiment toward the telephone company, and the relative importance of the company in the economy.

The case material, for example, showed that the Chilean Telephone Company (CTC) had a relatively short experience as a state-owned company. Furthermore, it was run like a private company during its tenure as a state-owned company; therefore, it never developed the network of interest groups that survived on rents derived from its operations. CTC always purchased its technology and equipment abroad; thus it did not breed a telecommunications industry that also depended on company rents for survival. Therefore, selling the company would not create much disturbance. Unfortunately, that was not true in the Brazilian and Argentine cases. Both countries developed extensive telecommunication industrial bases, with Brazil going one step further and developing a domestic technological format. Indeed, the case material showed that technology played an important role in shaping interest groups. The technological decisions made by some of the governments locked in the possibilities for interest group formation.

Interestingly, the power of interest groups to capture the national telephone company was not exclusive to Latin America. Other developing countries, such as India, had similar problems. In 1995, India attempted to privatize its state-owned telephone company, VSNL. However, powerful interest groups were able to block the initiative. In an embarrassing and destabilizing setback, the government was forced to abandon the sale of the company. Therefore, the information in the global database and case materials suggested that failure to take microeconomic, or company-level, factors into account when designing privatization policies could lead to dangerously wrong assumptions.

Macroeconomic Factors

The macroeconomic results were somewhat consistent with the expectations generated by the corresponding literature. The macroeconomic environment seemed to generate the underlying pressure, or incentives, to privatize.

An interesting insight uncovered by the analyses was that ideology had little do with the implementation of privatization policies. In fact, the cases showed that dire macroeconomic problems could push even the most ideologically opposed governments into the arms of privatization. This was definitely the case in 1990, when New Zealand's socialist government put NZ Telecom up for sale, and in 1994, when Fidel Castro sold a 49% stake in Emtel. This would appear to be counterintuitive at first glance; however, the breakdown of the Soviet regime at the end of the 1980s forced governments around the world to become more economically self-reliant.

One macroeconomic topic that deserves some further discussion is the role of foreign debt. The case material found that debt levels did not pressure governments to divest state-owned assets. Neither Brazil nor Argentina, both with ominous foreign debt obligations, cited debt as one of main driving factors to sell off its state-owned company. Therefore, this factor was not used in the statistical analysis. Yet, this conclusion may not be shared by some of the privatization initiatives launched in other parts of the world, particularly East Asia. For example, it is well known that the sales of the Pakistani Telephone Company (PTC) and Singapore Telecom (ST) were motivated by debt reduction concerns. Perhaps, since these economies already enjoyed high levels of growth and prudent fiscal management, thus the only remaining macroeconomic problems was the high level of foreign debt.

The macroeconomic section also found that the multilateral lending agencies played only a minimal role in the privatization process. Although multilateral lending agencies have often been accused of putting pressure on developing countries to privatize, the real pressures to sell have come from domestic factors. However, the study found one international force that had been somewhat ignored and could be the subject of future research. The role of international capital, in the form of multinational companies seeking to purchase privatized companies, is a factor that has been largely overlooked. This phenomenon may be categorized as the demand side of the privatization equation— in other words, what drove major telephone conglomerates to begin aggressively buying up state-owned telephone companies. Over a hundred years ago, developing countries were overrun by foreign investors. This influx reflected dynamic changes in telecommunications technology and the growing competition in home markets. A similar event is occurring again. Foreign investors are again offering to provide new technology to developing countries, but does this also mean that when the rate of telecommunications technological change slows down once more, as it did during the middle of the twentieth century, governments will be prone to renationalize these industries?

Political Factors

The political analyses produced some of the most interesting insights. The case studies showed that the power of the national executive was very important in determining whether a privatization would occur. Argentina's first attempt to sell Entel was blocked by the opposition. But when the opposition took over the presidency, it had the power to implement the sale. A similar event occurred in 1995, when Pakistan sold PTC. The sale was not implemented until Prime Minister Bhutto returned to power. Although she lacked a clear majority in the Parliament, she was able to implement the divestiture soon after her inauguration, during the honeymoon period. Other countries have decided to quietly table, or prolong, their privatization programs when they clearly lacked the political resources to implement the sale. This strategy prevents the embarrassment of abandoning the privatization process. For example, in 1994 and 1995, the Ecuadorian government expressed a strong desire to privatize its telephone company, Emtel. Yet, the administration lacked the political power to implement the sale. In fact, President Sixto Duran shared political affiliation with less than 2% of the Congress. This forced the government to postpone the divestiture, at least, until a more powerful national executive was elected. In 1995, the Turkish government also expressed an intent to sell off its state telephone unit, but the minority Çiller administration lacked the political resources to do so. Faced with tenuous political power, some governments, such as Russia (Rostelekom), South Korea (KT), and Portugal (PT), have decided to test the political waters by implementing a partial privatization of their state-owned telephone companies. These partial privatizations have allowed control to be retained by the state while generating new resources to address macroeconomic problems.

The case material, along with the statistical study of telecommunication privatizations throughout the world, produced several interesting and important observations and conclusions. One of the central findings from this study was that each of the individual factors shaping privatization initiatives does not provide a complete picture of the policy reforms, but *analyzed together* they provide a better understanding. It is clear that attempts by researchers to understand development phenomena without employing multidisciplinary factors may often result in incomplete explanations.

The intense focus on telephone companies allowed the creation of a virtual economic laboratory where I could test individual propositions in relative isolation from other factors. Other studies on privatization have examined the entire set of privatizations within a particular country or in the developing world. Most studies have examined just one case, or a few cases across different industries. However, no study has provided the detailed cross-sectional analysis of privatization in a single industry as this book does. By selecting a very precise topic and systematically analyzing the data and material through a broad spectrum of approaches, I have been able to arrive at a cohesive set of conclusions. In other words, by comparing oranges with oranges, an intricate level of understanding about a particular phenomenon has been achieved, thus allowing generalizations to be inferred about other countries and regions of the world.

The significance of this insight is important, not only for academic reasons but also due to the immense number of privatizations that are yet to come. The process of telephone privatization is only beginning. In addition to developing countries, such as Sri Lanka (SLT) and Uganda (UPTC), that have announced intentions to sell their state telephone companies after 1996, major European countries, such as France (France Telecom), Germany (Deutsche Telekom), and Italy (STET), have announced plans to divest their telecom giants. Furthermore, privatization is a process that is just beginning. Governments around the world still control hundreds of immense companies in strategic sectors, such as mining, oil, and utilities. All of these sectors contain powerful interest groups. Therefore, understanding the different dynamics that shape the privatization process will provide an important insight into the method of designing more efficient policies and creating better policy alternatives.

SELECTED BIBLIOGRAPHY

Abreu, Marcelo de Pavia and Rogério Werneck "Privatization and Regulation in Brazil: The 1990-1992 Policies and the Challenges Ahead" *Quarterly Review of Economics and Finance* 33 (1993): 21-44.

Acuña, Carlos "Politica Democratics y Cambio de Modelo de Acumulacion en la Argentina" *CEDES*, Presented at CEDES Conference on La Nueva Matriz Politica Argentina in Buenos Aires. November 26 and 27, 1993a.

Acuña, Carlos "Politics and Economics in Argentina in the Nineties" in William Smith's *Democracy, Markets and Structural Reforms in Latin America* New Brunswick: Transaction, 1993b.

Acuña, Carlos and Catalina Smulovitz "Militares en la Transicion Argentina: Del Gobierno a la Subordinacion Constitutional" CEDES, Presented at CEDES Conference on La Nueva Matriz Politica Argentina in Buenos Aires. November 26 and 27, 1993.

Alisky, Marvin *Uruguay: A Contemporary Survey* New York: Praeger, 1969.

Alsogaray, Maria Julia "Privatizacion de Entel" *Camara de Diputados de la Nacion*, Buenos Aires, 1990.

Alves, Maria Helena Moreira "Trade Unions in Brazil A Search for Autonomy and Organization" in Edward Epstein's (ed.) *Labor Autonomy and the State in Latin America* Boston: Unwin Hyman, 1989.

Angell, Alan, "Unions and Workers in Chile During the 1980s" in Drake, Paul and Ivan *Jaksic The Struggle for Democracy in Chile, 1982-1990* London: University of Nebraska Press, 1992.

ANTEL *En Sintesis* Montevideo, Uruguay 1992.

Armijo, Leslie *Balance Sheet or Ballot Box: Incentives to Privatize in Argentina, Mexico, Brazil, and India?* Boston: Northeastern University, 1994.

Arriagada, Genaro *Pinochet The Politics of Power* Boston: Unwin Hyman, 1988.

Austin, James, Lawrence Wortzel, and John Coburn "Privatizing State-Owned Enterprises: Hopes and Realities" *Columbia Journal of World Business* (Fall, 1986): 51-60.

Aylen, Jonathan "Privatization in Developing Countries" *Lloyds Bank Review* (1987).

Babai, Don "The World Bank and the IMF" Rolling Back the State or Backing its Role" in Raymond Vernon's (ed.) *The Promise of Privatization* New York: The Council on Foreign Relations, 1988.

Baer, Werner and Annibal Villela "Privatization and the Changing Role of the State in Brazil" Presented at the 17th LASA Conference in Los Angeles, California, September 24-27, 1992.

Bank for International Settlements *Annual Report* Basel, 1987.

Banks, Arthur "Brazil" *The Political Handbook of the World: 1993* New York: CSA Publications, 1993.

Bartell, Ernest "Privatization; The Role of Domestic Business" Helen Kellogg Institute for International Studies, University of Notre Dame, Working Paper #198, June 1993.

Beca, Raimundo *Privatization, Deregulation and Beyond: Trends in Telecommunication in Some Latin American Countries* Washington, D.C.: ECLAC, August 1991.

Beinen, Henry and John Waterbury "The Political Economy of Privatization in Developing Countries*" World Development* (1989): 617-632.

Blake II, Charles Henry *Social Pacts, Labor Relations and Democratic Consolidation: Argentina in Comparative Perspective* Ph.D. Dissertation, Duke University 1992.

BNDES *Legislacão Basica do Sistema BNDES, 1991* Rio de Janeiro: BNDES, 1991.

BNDES *The National Destatization Program* Rio de Janeiro, 1992.

Booz Allen & Hamilton *Estudio Para La Reestructuracion del Sector de Telecomunicaciones* Montevideo, Uruguay, 1991.

Bös, Dieter and Wolfgang Peters "Privatization of Public Enterprises: A Principal-Agent Approach Comparing Efficiency in Private and Public Sectors" *Empirica* 18, 1 (1991).

Brazil Service "Telebras Eurobond Issue" September 2, 1992.

Brock, Philip *If Texas were Chile: A Primer on Banking Reform* San Francisco: ICS Press, 1992.

Budnevich, Carlos "Implicancias Financieras de las Privatizaciones en Chile" CIEPLAN, mimeo, 1993.

Business Latin America "Take Three" April 26, 1993.

Business Latin America "Telebras has big plans" June 7, 1993.

Canitrot, Adolfo and Silvia Sigal "Economic Reform, Democracy and the Crisis of the State in Argentina" Buenos Aires: Instituto Di Tella, 1992 mimeo.

Cardoso, Eliana and Albert Fishlow *The Macroeconomics of Brazilian External Debt* Chicago: University of Chicago Press, 1988.

Cardoso, Eliana and Ann Helwege *Latin American Economy* Cambridge: MIT Press, 1992.

Cardoso, Eliana and Rudiger Dornbusch "Brazilian Debt Crises: Past and Present" in Barry Eichengreen and Peter Lindert's *The International Debt Crisis in Historical Perspective* Cambridge: MIT Press, 1991: 106-139.

Castillo, Mario "Privatizaciones De Empresas Publicas en Chile" El Caso del Sector Telecomunicaciones" mimeo, CEPAL, 1993.

CERES (Centro de Estudios de la Realidad Economica y Social) "El Proyecto de Desmonopolizacion" November, 1991.

Chernow, Ron *The House of Morgan* New York: Atlantic Monthly Press, 1990.

Cook, Paul and Colin Kirkpatrick *Privatization in Less Developed Countries* New York: St. Martin's Press 1988.

Cook, Paul and Martin Minogue "Waiting for Privatization in Developing Countries" *Public Administration and Development* 10 (1990): 389-403.

CS First Boston *Uruguay: A Diamond in the Rough* New York, 1994a.

CS First Boston. Conversations with telephone industry analysts, 1994b.

CTC, *Statistical Yearbook of Development in Telecommunications, 1960-1989* Santiago, Chile, 1990.

Damill, Mario, and Roberto Frenkel "Malos Tiempos: Argentina en la Decada de los Ochenta" CEDES, 1990.

Devlin, Robert "Las Privatizaciones y el Bienestar Social" *Revista CEPAL* Santiago, Chile, 1992.

Devlin, Robert *Debt and Crisis in Latin America* Princeton: Princeton University Press, 1989.

Diaz-Alejandro, Carlos *Essays on the Economic History of Argentina* New Haven: Yale University Press, 1970.

Dmytraczenko, Tania "Privatization of Telephones in Brazil" Ph.D. Dissertation University of North Carolina at Chapel-Hill, 1993.

Douglas, Roger "The Politics of Successful Structural Reform" *Wall Street Journal*, (January 26, 1990): 6.

Dromi, Jose Roberto *Reforma del Estado y Privatizaciones* Buenos Aires: Editorial Astrea de Alfredo y Ricardo DePlama, 1991.

Duch, Raymond *Privatizing the Economy: Telecommunications Policy in Comparative Perspective* Ann Arbor: The University of Michigan Press, 1991.

Durchslag, Scott, Tino Puri, and Arvind Rao "The Promise of Infrastructure Privatization" *The McKinsey Quarterly* No. 1, 1994.

EIU *Chile: Country Profile* London: Economist Intelligence Unit, 1987.

Euromoney "Guide to Brazil: Special Report" May, 1994.

Evans, Peter. *Dependent Development: The Alliance of Multinational, State and Local Capital in Brazil* Princeton: Princeton University Press, 1979.

Ffrench-Davis, Ricardo "El Conflicto Entre La Dueda y El Creciemento en Chile" *Coleccion Estudios CIEPLAN* 26, June 1989, pp. 61-89.

Filgueira, Fernando and Jorge Papadopulos "Putting Conservatism to Good Use? Long Crises and Vetoed Alternatives in Uruguay" presented at seminar :Inequality and New Forms of Representation in Latin America," Columbia University, New York, March 3-5, 1994.

Financial Times "Telebras turns in profits of Dollars 447m" November 17, 1992.

Fishlow, Albert "Conditionality and Willingness to Pay" in Barry Eichengreen and Peter Lindert's *The International Debt Crisis in Historical Perspective* (Cambridge: MIT Press, 1991), 86-105.

Fraja, Giovanni "Efficiency and Privatization in Imperfectly Competitive Industries" *Journal of Industrial Economics* 39, 3, (1991): 311-327.

Frieden, Jeffrey *Debt, Development, and Democracy: Modern Political Economy and Latin America, 1965-85* Princeton: Princeton University Press, 1991.

Galal, Ahmed, "Regulation, Commitment and Development of Telecommunications in Chile" World Bank Working Paper, April, 1993.

Gargiulo, Martin "The Uruguayan Labor Movement in the Post-Authoritarian Period" in Edward Epstein's *Labor Autonomy and the State in Latin America* Boston: Unwin Hyman, 1989.

Gaudio, Ricardo, Andres Thompson, and Luis Garcia Fanlo "El Moviemento Obrero Argentino en el Nuevo Escenario Democratico" CEDES, Presented at CEDES Conference on La Nueva Matriz Politica Argentina in Buenos Aires. November 26 and 27, 1993.

Geddes, Barbara *Politicians Dilemma: Building State Capacity in Latin America* London: University of California Press, 1994.

Gerchunoff, Pablo *Las Privatizaciones en la Argentina* Buenos Aires: Instituto Torcuato Di Tella, 1993.

Gil-Garcia, Olga "Structuring Telecommunications Markets From the USA and the Brazilian Perspectives" University of North Carolina at Chapel Hill, 1993, mimeo.

Giraldo, Jeanne "Development and Democracy in Chile: Finance Minister Alejandro Foxley and the Concertation Project for the 90s" Paper Presented at the Latin American Studies Association Conference, March 10-12, 1994, mimeo.

Glade, William "Privatization in Rent-Seeking Societies" *World Development* 17, 5 (1989): 673-682.

Glade, William *Privatization of Public Enterprises in Latin America* San Francisco: ICS Press, 1991.

Gomes, Eduardo "Business-State Relations in Brazil's Export-Oriented Growth" Paper for the XVIII International Congress, LAS, March 10-12, 1994, mimeo.

Gonzalez, Luis *Political Structures and Democracy in Uruguay* Notre Dame: Helen Kellogg Institute for International Studies, 1991.

Hachette, D. and R. Lüders "El Processo de Privatization en Chile desde 1984" *Boletin Econmico* no. 24, 1988.

Hachette, D. and R. Lüders "La Privatization en Chile" Santiago, Chile: *CINDE*, 1992.

Haggard, Stephan and Robert Kaufman "Institutions and Economic Adjustment" in *The Politics of Economic Adjustment* Princeton: Princeton University Press, 1992.

Haggard, Stephen and Steven Webb *Voting for Reform: Democracy, Political Liberalization and Economic Adjustment* New York: Oxford University Press, 1994.

Hagopian, Frances "Democracy by Undemocratic Means?" *Comparative Political Studies* Vol. 23, No. 2, July 1990.

Hanke, Steve *Privatization and Development* San Francisco: Institute for Contemporary Studies 1987.

Helena, Maria, and Moreira Alves "Trade Unions in Brazil" *Labor Autonomy and the State in Latin America* Boston: Unwin Hyman, 1989.

Hemming, Richard and Ali Mansoor *Privatization and Public Enterprises* Washington, D.C.: International Monetary Fund, 1988.

Herrera, Alejandra "La Privatizacion de la Telefonia Argentina" *Revista de la CEPAL* August, 1992.

Herrera, Alejandra *La Revolucion Tecnolgica y la Telefonia Argentina* Buenos Aires: Legasa, 1989.

Herrera, Alejandra and Ben Alfa Petrazzini "Technological Revolution, Regulation, and Privatization: Reach and Limits of the Argentine Case" Paper presented at Columbia University, New York, 1992.

Hill, Alice and Manuel Angel Abdala "Regulation, Institutions and Commitment" April 8, 1993, mimeo.

Hobday, Michael *Telecommunications in Developing Countries: The Challenge From Brazil* New York: Routledge, 1990.

Horowitz, Donald "Comparing Democratic Systems" *Journal of Democracy* 1, 4 (Fall, 1990): 73-91.

Hoy, "Chicago Boys: La Historia No Contada" 17 September 1984.

IADB (Inter-Amercan Development Bank) *Annual Report* Washington, D.C. 1992.

Iazzetta, Osvaldo Miguel "Reforma Politica y Partidos Politicos" Presented at Primer Congresso de la Sociedad Argentina de Analisis Politico, Buenos Aires, Argentina, November, 1993.

Ikenberry, John "The International Spread of Privatization Policies: Inducements, Learning and 'Policy Bandwagoning'" in E. Suleiman and J. Waterbury's *The Political Economy of Public Sector Reform and Privatization* Boulder: Westview, 1993.

Institutional Investor "The $100 Billion Telecom Bonanza" (June, 1992): 35.

International Institute of Finance *Argentina* Washington, D.C. August 1992

International Institute of Finance *Brazil* Washington, D.C. September 1992

International Institute of Finance *Chile* Washington, D.C. June 1992

International Institute of Finance *Uruguay* Washington, D.C. January 1994

ITU, *Americas Telecommunications Indicator Database* World Bank, 1992.

ITU, *Americas Telecommunications Indicator Database* World Bank, 1995.

Jatoba, Jorge "Labor and Economic Reform in Brazil" mimeo LASA, 1994.

Jones, Leroy, Pankaj Tandon and Ingo Vogelsang *Selling Public Enterprises* Boston: MIT Press, 1990.

Kahler, Miles "External Influence, Conditionality, and the Politics of Adjustment" in Stephen Haggard and Robert Kaufman's *The Politics of Economic Adjustment* Princeton: Princeton University Press, 1992.

Kahler, Miles "International Actors and the Politics of Adjustment" in Joan Nelson, ed., *The Fragile Politics of Adjustment* Washington, D.C., Overseas Development Council, 1989.

Kelsey, Sarah, and Steve Levitsky "Captivating Alliances: Unions, Labor-Backed Parties, and the Politics of Economic Liberalization in Argentina and Mexico" Paper Presented at the LASA XVIII, Atlanta, Georgia, March 10-12, 1994.

Kimenyi, Mwangi, and John Mbaku "Rent Seeking and Institutional Stability in Developing Countries" *Public Choice* 77, 385-405, 1993.

King, Gary, Robert Keohane, and Sidney Verba *Designing Social Inquiry: Scientific Inference in Qualitative Research* Princeton: Princeton University Press, 1994.

Koehnlein, Bill "Lula: A Political Biography" New York: Brecht Forum, 1994, mimeo.

Lal, Deepak and Sylvia Maxfield "The Political Economy of Stabilization in Brazil" in Robert Bates and Anne O. Krueger's *Political and Economic Interactions in Economic Policy Reform* Oxford, U.K.: Blackwell, 1993.

Langevin, Mark "Development by Division: The Brazilian Labor Movement" LASA mimeo, 1994.

Larrain, Felipe "The Economic Challenges of Democratic Development" in Drake, Paul and Ivan Jaksic (eds.) *The Struggle for Democracy in Chile, 1982-1990* London: University of Nebraska Press, 1992.

Latin America Weekly Report "Bid to open up telecoms market"; November 22, 1990.

Latin American Newsletters "Brazil's battle for control of industrial technology" July 28, 1978.

Latin American Weekly Report "More Rows Looming in Mercosur" May 13, 1993.

Latin Finance "Privatization in Latin America" March 1992.

Lerner, N.C. "Telecommunications Privatization and Liberalization in Developing Countries" *Telecommunications Journal* 58 (1991): 279-286.

Levy, Brian and Pablo Spiller "Regulation, Institutions and Commitment in Telecommunications" Washington, D.C.: World Bank Papers, 1993.

Lewis, Paul, *The Crisis of Argentine Capitalism* London: University of North Carolina-Chapel Hill Press, 1990.

Leyden, Patrick and Albert Link "Privatization, Bureaucracy, and Risk Aversion" *Public Choice* 76 (1993): 199-213.

Linz, Juan "The Perils of Presidentialism" *Journal of Democracy* 1, 1 (Winter, 1990): 51-69.

Mainwaring, Scott "Presidentialism, Multipartism, and Democracy" *Comparative Political Studies* 26, 2, (July 1993): 198-220.

Mainwaring, Scott *Dilemmas of Multiparty Presidential Democracy: The Case of Brazil* Notre Dame: University of Notre Dame Press, 1994.

Mann, Catherine, Stefanie Lenway, and Derek Utter "Political and Economic Consequences of Alternative Privatization Strategies" *International Finance*

Discussion Papers Washington, D.C.: Board of Governors of the Federal Reserve System, Number 455, September 1993.

Manzetti, Luigi "Economic Reform and Corruption in Latin America" *North-South Issues* Vol. 3, No. 1, 1994.

Manzetti, Luigi "The Political Economy of Privatization through Divestiture in Lesser Developed Economies" *Comparative Politics* (July 1993): 429-455.

Marcel, Mario "Privatizacion y Finanzas Publicas: El Caso de Chile, 1985-1988" *Coleccion Estudios CIEPLAN* No. 26, June 1989, pp. 5-60.

Martin, Lisa *Coercive Cooperation* Princeton: Princeton University Press, 1994.

Mayer, Colin and Shirley Meadowcroft "Selling Public Assets" *Fiscal Studies* 6, 4 (1986): 42-56.

McDonald, Ronald "The Dilemma of Normalcy in Uruguay" *Current History* 1988.

Meller, Patricio "A Review of the Chilean Privatization Experience" mimeo, CIEPLAN, Chile 1992.

Melo, Jose Ricardo "Panorama de las Telecommunicaciones en Chile" Draft Universidad de Chile, May 1992.

Mendes, Julio Cesar "Ima Anaise do Programa Brasileiro de Privatizacão" *Conjuntura* Vol. 41, No. 9, 1987.

Mericle, Kenneth S. Corporatist Control of the Working Class: Authoritarian Brazil since 1964." *Authoritarianism and Corporatism in Latin America* in James Malloy's (ed.), 303-38 Pittsburgh: University Pittsburgh Press, 1977.

Mora y Araujo, Manuel *Ensayo y Error* Buenos Aires: Planeta, 1991.

Murillo, Victoria "Unions and Privatization in Argentina" Harvard, 1994, mimeo.

Nankani, Helen "Lessons of Privatization in Developing Countries" *Finance and Development* (March 1990).

Nellis, John and Sunita Kikeri "Public Enterprises Reform: Privatization and the World Bank" *World Development* 17, 5 (May, 1989): 659-672.

Nelson, Joan *Economic Crisis and Policy Adjustment in the Third World* Princeton: Princeton University Press, 1990.

Nelson, Joan *Economic Crisis and Policy Choice: The Politics of Adjustment in the Third World* Princeton: Princeton University Press, 1990.

O'Donnell, Guillermo and Phillippe Schmitter's *Transitions from Authoritarian Rule: Comparative Perspectives* Baltimore: John Hopkins University Press, 1986.

Olson, Mancur, Jr. *The Logic of Collective Action* Cambridge: Cambridge University Press, 1971.

Önis, Ziya "Privatization and the Logic of Coalition Building: A Comparative Analysis of State Divestiture in Turkey and the United Kingdom" *Comparative Political Studies* 24, 2, (July 1991).

Ott, Attiat *Privatization and Economic Efficiency* London: Edward Elgar Publishing, 1991.

Packenham, Robert "The Politics of Economic Liberalization: Argentina and Brazil in Comparative Perspective" Helen Kellogg Institute for International Studies, University of Notre Dame, Working Paper #206, April 1994.

Payne, Leigh *Brazilian Industrialists and Democratic Change* London: Johns Hopkins University Press, 1994.

Pereira, Luiz Carlos Bresser Pereira "Brazil" in John Williamson's *The Political Economy of Policy Reform* Washington: D.C., Institute for International Economics, 1994.

Petrazzini, Ben, "The Privatization of Telecommunications in Argentina" in Ravi Ramamurti's *Privatization of Infrastructure* Washington, D.C.: Brookings Institute Press, 1993.

Petrecolla, Alberto, Alberto Porto, and Pablo Gerchunoff "Privatization in Argentina" Presented at Latin America 2000 Conference, November 1992, University of Illinois at Urbana-Champaign.

Pietrobelli, Carlos "Trade Liberalization and Industrial Response: The Case of Chile" (1974-1987), LASA Conference March 1994, mimeo.

Pinheiro, Armando and Ben Ross Schneider *The Fiscal Impact of Privatization in Latin America* Austin, Texas: Latin America 2000 Conference, 1993.

Power, Timothy "The Pen is Mightier than the Congress: Presidential Decree Power in Brazil" presented at LASA XVIII on March 10-12, 1994, mimeo.

Przeworski, Adam *Democracy and the Market* Cambridge: Cambridge University Press, 1991.

Przeworski, Adam "Some Problems in the Study of the Transition to Democracy" *Transitions from Authoritarian Rule* in Guillermo O'Donnell's (ed.) Baltimore: Johns Hopkins University Press, 1986.

Rabkin, Rhoda "The Lessons of Chile: Economic Expertise, Social Learning, and the Consolidation of Market Reforms" presented at 18th International LASA Congress, Atlanta, Georgia, March 10-12, 1994. Mimeo.

Ramamurti, Ravi "The Impact of Privatization on the Latin American Debt Problem" *Journal of Interamerican Studies and World Affairs* 34, 2 (Summer 1992): 93-126 .

Ramamurti, Ravi "Why Are Developing Countries Privatizing?" *Journal of International Business Studies*. Vol. 23 No. 2, 1992.

Resende-Santos, Joao "Fernando Henrique Cardoso: Fighting for Democracy and Social Justice in Brazil" Department of Government, Harvard, 1994, mimeo.

Ritter, A.R.M. "Development Strategy and Structural Adjustment in Chile, 1973-1990" *Canadian Journal of Latin American and Caribbean Studies* Vol. 15, No. 30, pp. 159-175.

Ruiz-Tagle, Jaime "Trade Unionism and the State Under the Chilean Military Regime" in Edward Epstein's *Labor Autonomy and the State in Latin America* Boston: Unwin Hyman, 1989.

Sachs, Jeffrey "Conditionality, Debt Relief, and the Developing Country Debt Crisis" *Developing Country Debt and Economic Performance* Chicago: University of Chicago Press, 1989: 255-298.

Sáez, Raul "Las Privatizaciones de Empressas en Chile" CIEPLAN, 1992, mimeo.

Salomon Brothers "Telebras S.A.–High Expectations" Emerging Markets Research, June 1993.

Sampson, Anthony *The Sovereign States of ITT* New York, Stein and Day, 1973.

Sandholtz, Wayne. "Institutions and Collective Action: The New Telecommunications in Western Europe" *World Politics* (January 1993): 242-271.

Savas, E.S. *The Key to Better Government* New York: Chatham House, 1987.

Scalabrini, Raul *Historia de los Ferrocarriles Argentinos* Buenos Aires: Reconquista, 1940.

Schattschneider, Elmer *The Semisovereign People* Hinsdale, Illinois: Dryden Press, 1960.

Schneider, B. "Partly for Sale: Privatization and State Strength in Brazil and Mexico" *Journal of Interamerican Studies and World Affairs* 30, 4 (Winter 1989): 89-116.

Schneider, Ben Ross "Privatization in the Collor Government: Triumph of Liberalism or Collapse of the State" in Douglas Chalmers, Maria do Carmo Campello and Atilio Boron's (eds.) *The Right and Democracy in Latin America* New York: Praeger, 1992: 225-238.

Schoenberg, Robert *Geneen* New York: Norton & Company, 1985.

Scully, Timothy *Rethinking the Center: Party Politics in 19th and 20th Century Chile* Stanford: Stanford University Press, 1992.

Senado de la Nacion *Diario de Asuntos Entrados* Lunes 2 de Enero, Buenos Aires, 1989: 12.

Shugart, Matthew, and John Carey *Presidents and Assemblies: Constitutional Design and Electoral Dynamics* New York: Cambridge University Press, 1992.

Sigmund, P. "Privatization, Reprivatization, Hyperprivatization" *Privatization Workshop* Princeton University, 1988.

Silva, Eduardo "The Political Economy of Chile's Regime Transition: From Radical to Pragmatic Neo-Liberal Policies" in Paul Drake and Ivan Jaksic's (eds.)*The Struggle for Democracy in Chile, 1982-1990* London: University of Nebraska Press, 1992.

Skidmore, Thomas *Politics in Brazil* New York: Oxford University Press, 1967.

Smith, William "State, Market and Neoliberalism in Post-Transition Argentina: The Menem Experiment" *Journal of Interamerican Studies and World Affairs* Vol. 33, 1991.

Snow, Peter *Political Forces in Argentina* New York: Praeger, 1979. p. 23.

Souto, Marcos Juruena "O Programa Brasileiro de Privatizacão de Empresas Estatais" *Revista de Dieito Mercantil Industrial, Economico e Financeiro* No. 80, October 1990.

Stallings, Barbara and Phillip Brock "Political Economy of Economic Adjustment: Chile, 1973-90" in Robert Bates and Anne Krueger *Political and Economic Interactions in Economic Policy Reform* Cambridge: Blackwell, 1993: 78-122.

Stepan, Alfred "Political Leadership and Regime Breakdown: Brazil" in Juan Linz and Alfred Stepan's (eds.) *The Breakdown of Democratic Regimes* Johns Hopkins University Press, 1978.

Stepan, Alfred, "Paths Toward Redemocratization" in Guillermo O'Donnell and Phillippe Schmitter's (eds.) *Transitions from Authoritarian Rule: Comparative Perspectives* Baltimore: Johns Hopkins University Press, 1986.

Strom, Kaare "Minority Governments in Parliamentary Democracies" *Comparative Political Studies* Vol. 17, No. 4: 199-227, 1984.

Teixeira, Nelson Carlos "Perspectives and Preferences Regarding Privatization Policies in Brazil" Doctoral Dissertation, University of Pittsburgh, 1989.

Telebras "Planning Documents" mimeo Rio de Janiero, 1977.

Telebras *1990 Annual Report* Brasilia, Brazil 1990.

Telebras *1991 Annual Report* Brasilia, Brazil 1991.

Telephony "Formidable Aspirations Lead Brazil Forward" October 24, 1988.

The Economist "Brazilian telephones; Hang on" August 16, 1986.

The Political Handbook of the World: 1993 New York: CSA Publications, 1995.

United Press International "IMF Will Continue Lending to Countries with Arrears to Banks" Washington, D.C.: UPS, September 21, 1989.

Vernon, Raymond. *The Promise of Privatization* New York: Council on Foreign Relations, 1988.

Waisman, Carlos "The Argentine Paradox" *Journal of Democracy* (1990): pp. 32-40.

Wajnberg, Salomao "Accesso ao Mercado Barrieras e Expectativas: O Caso do Brasil" Brasilia: Ministerio das Communicacaoes, 1992. mimeo.

Wajnberg, Salomáo "La Industria de Equipos de Telecomunicaciones en Brasil" *Integracion Latinoamericana* March, 1990.

Waterbury, John "The Heart of the Matter? Public Enterprise and the Adjustment Process" in Stephen Haggard and Robert Kaufman's *The Politics of Economic Adjustment* Princeton: Princeton University Press, 1992.

Weinstein, Martin *Uruguay: Democracy at the Crossroads* London: Westview Press, 1988.

Wellenius, Bjorn *Telecommunications and Economic Development* Washington, D.C.: The World Bank and Johns Hopkins University Press, 1994.

Wellenius, Bjorn and Peter Stern *Implementing Reforms in the Telecommunications Sector* Washington, D.C.: The World Bank and Johns Hopkins University Press, 1994.

Wellons, Paul *Passing the Buck: Banks, Governments, and Third World Debt* Boston: Harvard Business School Press, 1987.

Williamson, John *IMF Conditionality* Washington, D.C.: Institute for International Economics, 1983.

World Bank *Uruguay: The Private Sector* Washington, D.C.: World Bank, 1994.

World Bank *World Debt Tables* Washington, D.C.: World Bank, 1992.

Yotopoulos, Pan "The (Rip)Tide of Privatization: Lessons from Chile" *World Development* Vol. 17, No. 5, 1989.

INDEX

About the Author

WALTER T. MOLANO is Director of Economic and Financial Research at Swiss Bank Corporation. He received his Ph.D. in Economic Development and Finance and has done extensive research in the area of privatization, focusing mainly on South America.

ISBN 0-313-30055-0
EAN
9 780313 300554

HARDCOVER BAR CODE